BERLITZ®

FLORENCE

- A ✓ in the text denotes a highly recommended sight
- A complete A–Z of practical information starts on p.105
- Extensive mapping on cover flaps

Printed in Switzerland by Weber SA, Bienne.

1st Edition (1995/1996)

Although we make every effort to ensure the accuracy of the information in this guide, changes do occur. If you have any new information, suggestions or corrections to contribute, we would like to hear from you. Please write to Berlitz Publishing at the above address.

Text:	Neil Wilson
Editors:	Donald Greig; Olivier and Isabelle Fleuraud
Photography:	Jon Davison
Layout:	Suzanna Boyle
Cartography:	Visual Image
Thanks to:	The Italian Tourist Office (ENIT) for their help in the preparation of this guide.

Cover photographs: (front) *Florence skyline*; (back) *Ponte Vecchio and the River Arno* © Tony Stone Photolibrary – London

CONTENTS

Florence and the Florentines

The magnificent view from the hilltop church of San Miniato has changed little since the 16th century. It looks out across the brick-red rooftops of Florence, a sea of terracotta tiles interrupted only by the hulking domes of San Lorenzo and the Duomo, and the fairy-tale tower of the Palazzo Vecchio. Here, the past feels very close. With a little imagination, it's easy to transport yourself back to the time of the Renaissance, when this small Tuscan town was one of the most important cities in Europe.

Florence is unique. The massive contribution it has made to Western civilization and culture is out of all proportion to its diminutive size. Few nations, let alone cities, can boast of having nurtured such an overpowering array of artistic, literary, and political talent in so short a period of time. The names of Florence's greatest sons – Michelangelo, Dante, Boccaccio, Giotto, Donatello, Botticelli, Leonardo, Cellini and Machiavelli – are famous the world over; it is an incredible record for a city whose period of greatness spanned less than 300 years.

Guidebooks often compare Renaissance Florence with 5th-century BC Athens, but while the glory that was Greece is recalled only by spectacular ruins, Florence remains very much alive. Its historic palaces, great churches, fine sculptures and works of art are not crumbling relics, but still a functional part of everyday life – worked in, lived in, prayed in, and prized by present-day Florentines – accessible to all.

The Palazzo Vecchio, where the first civic authority sat in the Middle Ages, still houses the offices of the city council. Congregations kneel to say Mass in the churches where medieval merchants knelt before them. The cantilevered shops on the Ponte Vecchio are still occupied by goldsmiths, who first set up workshops here in the 14th century. Most of the city's streets are as narrow, and their paving as uneven, as they were three centuries ago. The dishes on the menu of a Florentine restaurant would be familiar to a 16th-century cook, and the babble of voices filling a Florentine bar would still sound familiar to Dante.

Time, of course, has not stood still. The narrow streets are plagued with traffic, and TV aerials sprout from the red-tiled roofs. The greatest impetus towards change, however, has been tourism. Ever since the late 18th century, when Florence and its treasures became part of the 'Grand Tour' undertaken by the British gentry, the city has proved irresistible to tourists.

Today, the medieval alleys are lined with ice-cream bars and pizza parlours, while post-card vendors and souvenir stalls crowd the piazzas, and milling throngs of visitors from around the world – Europe, America and Japan – cram the streets and passageways.

Those who are uncomfortable with Florence describe it as overcrowded, overpowering and overpriced, and there is undeniably some truth in such criticisms. The crowds, and to a certain extent the high prices, can be avoided by visiting in low season. Whenever you go, though, there is no escaping the overwhelming impact of so much superlative art and architecture, especially when you may have only a few days to see it. The answer is to be se-

The cafés and news-stands of the Piazza della Repubblica lie at the heart of modern-day Florence.

lective: pick out a few highlights and absorb them at your leisure (see p.23). If you try to cover everything, you'll end up enjoying nothing.

The medieval Florentines were described as pragmatic, hard-working, inventive, and sharp-witted. These qualities are still evident in today's inhabitants, along with an inborn sense of dignity and elegance, a biting, often cruel wit and a savage pride in their city.

You may find them disappointingly 'un-Italian' in their behaviour; as a whole they're less forthcoming with strangers than, say, the Neapolitans or Romans – they're courteous but won't pander to your whims. You'll experience little of the traditional Italian exuberance, except perhaps for the occasional exchange of street insults delivered in the thick Tuscan accent.

Florentines are also renowned for their remarkable resilience. This has been illustrated repeatedly throughout history, but no more effectively so than during the disastrous flood of November 1966 (the worst of around 50 floods experienced by the city) when,

Florence is home to some of the finest art ever produced by Western civilization.

swollen by heavy rains, the Arno burst its banks one night, carrying all before it. In certain parts of the city, the water reached depths of 7m (23ft). Thick mud, as well as oil from ruptured central-heating tanks, swirled into basements, cellars and ground-floor rooms. Hundreds of paintings, frescoes and sculptures, and over a million priceless antique books suffered incalculable damage.

Even before the flood waters had receded, the people of Florence rose to the challenge and joined in the task of rescuing what they could. In the aftermath, they helped with the work of clearing debris and repairing the urban fabric, and with the hard job of restoring damaged paintings and sculptures. While some restoration continues, most works have been repaired and are once again on display in the city museums and galleries.

The people's resolve was tested once again in May 1993, when a terrorist bomb tore apart the west wing of the Uffizi Gallery. Almost before the dust had settled, repairs were under way. The Uffizi's 150 members of staff worked round the clock without extra pay, putting the building back in order as soon as possible. As a result, most of the gallery was re-opened to the public less than two months later.

It is this sense of being custodians of the legacy of the

Renaissance, and heir to a great tradition of excellence, that gives the Florentines such fierce pride in their city. The subsequent feeling of continuity with the past is what makes Florence such an evocative place for the visitor. The paintings, sculptures and other splendid works of art are not viewed simply as isolated museum pieces, but in the context of the city that produced them. They are a living record of an extraordinary period of creativity and innovation.

For this alone, Florence deserves all the superlatives that are heaped upon it. What's more, if the heat, crowds, and queues become too much, you can always escape to that hilltop across the river, and savour the same view that Michelangelo must have savoured four and a half centuries ago.

The surrounding hills offer a pleasant escape from the heat and bustle of the city.

A Brief History

No one quite knows how the Roman town of Florentia came by its name. According to some, it was named after Florinus, a Roman general, who in 63 BC encamped on the city's future site in order to besiege the nearby Etruscan hill town of Fiesole. Others maintain that it referred to the abundance of flowers in the region, or perhaps even to the 'flourishing' of the successful town.

Whatever the origin of its name, Roman Florence developed into a thriving military and commercial settlement in around 59 BC. If you take a walk along Via Romana and cross the famous Ponte Vecchio towards the city centre, you'll be following in the steps of the Roman legions, travellers and merchants of two thousand years ago. And even though you'll find no visible Roman remains in Florence, all the trappings of civilized Roman life were once located here, including a forum, baths, temples and a theatre.

However, a few centuries later, barbarian invasions and the fall of the Roman empire plunged Europe into a dark and turbulent period of history. A ray of light shone briefly during the sway of Charlemagne's vast European empire of the 8th and 9th centuries, but by the 10th century even greater chaos had set in.

Somehow the Carolingian province of Tuscany survived. In the late 11th century, Florence made rapid commercial and political progress under a remarkable ruler, Matilda, the Margrave of Tuscany. The great guilds (*arti maggiore*) – influential bodies set up to protect the interests of the apothecaries, and the wool, silk and spice merchants – came into being, and by 1138, just 23 years after Matilda's death, Florence had developed into a self-governing republic and a power to be reckoned with.

At that time, the city presented a very different appearance from that of today. The wealthy merchant families built square stone towers (often more than 70m/230ft high)

HISTORICAL LANDMARKS

59 BC	Roman colony of Florentia founded by Julius Caesar.
3rd cen. AD	Population of Florentia reaches 10,000 inhabitants.
541-44	Byzantine city walls erected.
552	City falls to the invading Goths, and later comes under Lombard dominion.
8th-9th cen.	Florence is part of Charlemagne's empire; Carolingian city walls built.
1115	The *Comune* of Florence is granted the status of an independent city.
12th cen.	Rise of Florence as a commercial power.
13th cen.	Struggle for power between the Guelph and Ghibelline factions. Santa Croce founded by the Franciscans, Santa Maria Novella by the Dominicans.
c. 1240	The Florentine unit of currency, the florin, becomes the standard gold coin in European commerce.
1284-1333	Construction of outer city walls.
1290-1375	Alighieri, Petrarch and Boccaccio lay the foundations of modern Italian language and literature.
1347-48	Black Death wipes out half of Florence's population.
1434-64	Cosimo de' Medici (Il Vecchio) becomes the first Medici ruler of Florence.
1464-69	Piero Il Gottoso ('the Gouty') succeeds his father, Cosimo de' Medici, as ruler of the city.
1469-92	Lorenzo Il Magnifico succeeds his father, Piero Il Gottoso.
1494-98	'Theocratic republic' of Girolamo Savonarola ends with his public execution in Piazza della Signoria.
1737	Death of Anna Maria de' Medici, last of the Medici.
1861	Unification of Florence with the newly formed kingdom of Italy.
1865-71	Florence is the provisional capital of Italy.
1966	Widespread devastation caused by one of the worst floods in the city's history.
1993	Uffizi Gallery damaged by a terrorist bomb.

onto their houses, to serve as impregnable refuges during the recurring feuds that split the community. By the end of the 12th century, the city's skyline bristled with over 150 towers, although none has survived. (Some idea of the town's early appearance can be gained, however, by visiting San Gimignano; see p.85.)

Roman ruins (below) and Etruscan bronzes (right) attest to the long history of the region.

GUELPHS AND GHIBELLINES

Sooner or later the interests of an aristocratic elite and a rising merchant class were bound to clash, and when they did, Florence's development declined into a series of savage factional struggles. The nobility opposed the broader based forms of government that the merchants sought to promote, and the situation was aggravated by fierce inter-family feuds and continual raids on Florentine trade by 'robber barons'.

To make matters worse, powerful foreign interests became involved. The Guelph and Ghibelline parties, which developed in the 13th century, had their origins outside Florence, where the ambitions of the Papacy and the Holy Roman Empire were diverging dangerously – the Guelphs supported the Pope, while the Ghibellines took the side of the Emperor. Further complicating matters was the French monarchy, which took an especially keen interest in Florentine developments, and was always ready to interfere in – and profit from – the internecine strife.

Other Tuscan cities soon followed suit with their own Guelph-Ghibelline faction and Tuscany remained in a state of turmoil for over two centuries, as first the aristocratic Ghibellines, and then the merchant Guelphs gained the upper hand. Defeated leaders were exiled with their families and followers, and their property confiscated or destroyed. From the shelter of a friendly city, they would carefully plot their revenge, and the whole sorry cycle would begin once more. Pisa, Lucca, Pistoia, Siena, Arezzo, and Florence became in turn enemies or allies, depending on which party held power in which town.

Yet in spite of these setbacks, Florentine commerce and banking continued to develop and its woollen-cloth trade prospered. The first gold florin was minted in the mid-13th century, and was rapidly adopted throughout Europe as the standard unit of currency.

The city's social evolution during this time was also remarkable: organized 'factories' or workshops were opened; hospitals, schools and charitable societies were founded; the university (one of Europe's oldest) turned out lawyers, teachers and doctors by the score; streets were paved, and laws were passed regulating noise and nuisance; and the Brotherhood of the Misericordia, a forerunner of the Red Cross (see p.28) was established.

Although life was hard and Florence was never a democracy in the modern sense of the word, the city gave its citizens a unique sense of 'belonging' that overcame class or party differences.

In spite of their internal divisions, the Guelphs gradually edged the Ghibellines out of power. By the late 13th century, the bankers, merchants and city guilds had a firm grasp on the helm of the Florentine republic, and felt secure enough to turn their attention to the building of a fitting seat of government. With a sumptuous cathedral under construction, a mighty People's Palace – the Palazzo del Popolo – was

Florence's religious heart, the Piazza del Duomo, provides a dramatic setting for processions.

begun in 1298. This was later called the Palazzo della Signoria and is now known as the Palazzo Vecchio, which still serves as the city hall.

DAWN OF A GOLDEN AGE

Florentine bankers now held the purse-strings of Europe, with agents in every major city. One group, headed by the Bardi and Peruzzi families, lent Edward III of England 1,365,000 gold florins to finance his campaigns against the French. Yet, in 1343, the double-dealing Edward suddenly declared himself bankrupt, and toppled the entire banking system.

As always, the resilient Florentines recovered, and the merchant interests set out with ruthless zeal to regain their lost prestige. Despite ceaseless social unrest, violent working-class riots, disastrous floods and the Black Death of 1347-48 which claimed half the city's population, by the early 1400s Florence found itself stronger and richer than ever.

At the same time, the city's cultural life was flourishing, moving towards the early years of what was to become the Renaissance. Interest in long-neglected Greek and Latin literature was being revived; and while Florentine historians had started recording their city's progress for posterity, merchant guilds and the *nouveau riche* with money to burn – or guilty consciences to appease – found time between business deals and party vendettas to indulge in artistic patronage.

Despite factional divisions, the Florentines were able to plan ambitious public works and imposing private palaces – the Duomo, Giotto's Campanile, the great monastic churches of Santa Croce and Santa Maria Novella, the Bargello, and the Palazzo Vecchio were all begun or completed during the tumultuous 14th century.

The power of the important business families, the *signori*, proved greater than that of the guilds. The way now lay open for the ambitious Medici family of wealthy wool merchants and bankers to dominate every facet of Florentine life for 60 golden years (1434-94). They were shrewd politicians and enthusiastic and discerning patrons of the arts, and led the city and its people to unparalleled heights of civilization, at a time when most of Europe was struggling to free itself from the coarse, tangled mesh of medieval feudalism.

THE RENAISSANCE

The term 'Renaissance' was coined by the 16th-century Florentine artist, Giorgio Vasari (1511-74), whose book *Lives of the most excellent painters, sculptors and architects* makes fascinating reading and tells almost everything we know about the great Italian artists from the 13th century up to his own time.

Renaissance means rebirth, which is exactly how Vasari

The Renaissance period saw a flowering of creative energy – the pursuit of beauty for its own sake.

saw the events of the 15th century – the world appeared to be waking from a long sleep and taking up life where antiquity had left off.

The Church had dominated the cultural life of Europe throughout the Middle Ages. Literature, architecture, painting, sculpture and music were all aimed at the glorification of God, rather than the celebration of earthly life and beauty. The Greek and Roman concept of 'art for art's sake' had been forgotten until it was revived in 15th-century Florence. As you visit the Uffizi Gallery, compare Cimabue's *Virgin Enthroned* (c.1290) with Botticelli's *Primavera* (1477-78), which illustrate well the difference between the the Middle Ages and the Renaissance art.

In those uncertain times, the idea took hold that life must be lived to its fullest and that the

pursuit of earthly knowledge, beauty and pleasure were what counted in the brief time allotted to man. The arts and sciences of the Renaissance were directed towards those ends.

The Renaissance was dismissed by a 19th-century German scholar as 'an intellectual bacchanalia', but Lorenzo de' Medici – who was dubbed *Il Magnifico* for his patronage of art and scholarship – summed it up with greater charm:

Quant'è bella giovinezza,
che si fugge tuttavia!
Chi vuol esser lieto sia:
di doman non c'è certezza.

How fine a thing is youth
but how short-lived.
Let he who wishes to be
merry, be so.
For there's no saying what
tomorrow will bring.

The author of these noble sentiments had seen his 25-year-old brother Giuliano savagely murdered at his side by members of the rival Pazzi family, during Mass in the Duomo in 1478.

THE MEDICI INFLUENCE

Although few of the early Medici ever held office in the city government, three of them were in fact the true rulers of Florence. They were: Cosimo Il Vecchio ('the Elder', 1389-1464), a munificent patron of the arts and letters, who earned himself the title *pater patriae* ('father of his country'); his son, Piero Il Gottoso ('the Gouty', 1416-69); and his grandson Lorenzo Il Magnifico ('the Magnificent', 1449-92). Ably pulling strings via supporters elected to the republican government (the *Signoria*), all three were expert politicians who knew how to win the hearts and minds of the Florentine masses.

Poet, naturalist, art collector, dabbler in philosophy and would-be architect – a typical 'Renaissance man' – Lorenzo Il Magnifico was perhaps the most outstanding member of the Medici dynasty. His diplomatic skill kept Italy temporarily free of wars and invasions.

On Lorenzo's death in 1492, his son Piero took his place. Loutish and devoid of taste, Piero was totally unworthy of the Medici name; he lasted only two years. When Charles VIII of France invaded Italy, Piero first opposed him but suddenly changed sides as it became clear that the French were winning. He had to accept humiliating terms of settlement. The Florentine people were so enraged that they drove him from the city and set up a republic. It was at this time that Niccolo Machiavelli held office in Florence, gaining first-hand experience in the arts of intrigue and diplomacy.

The spiritual force behind the new republic was a fanatical Dominican friar, Girolamo Savonarola (1452-98), who had preached regularly in the Duomo during Lorenzo's last years. Audiences of thousands heard him inveigh against the excesses of the Medici, prophesying apocalyptic punishments for the city if its people did not embrace a more godly way of life. In 1494, he decreed the destruction of the 'vanities' of art, and Florentines flocked to the Piazza della Signoria with armfuls of books and paintings, which they hurled upon a huge bonfire in the middle of the square. Even Botticelli joined in, flinging some of his own paintings into the flames. But Savonarola had powerful enemies (pope Borgia, for one) who brought about his downfall. He was arrested, sentenced to death for heresy, and hanged and burned where his 'bonfire of the vanities' had taken place four years earlier.

In 1512, Piero's brothers, Giovanni and Giuliano, returned to Florence, putting an end to the republic. Expelled in 1527, the persistent Medici were back three years later, after an eight-month siege, with the help of the Holy Roman Emperor Charles V.

During the subsequent rule of grand-duke Cosimo I de' Medici from 1537 to 1574, an attempt was made to revive the spirit of the earlier Medicean golden age. Some of Florence's most prominent monuments date from this period, including the Santa Trinita Bridge, Boboli Gardens, the Neptune Fountain in the Piazza della Signoria, and Cellini's magnificent bronze *Perseus* in the Loggia dei Lanzi.

Florentine Explorers

AMERIGO VESPUCCI (1454-1512) went down in history as the man who gave his name to America. Banker, businessman and navigator, he crossed the Atlantic in the wake of Christopher Columbus, and explored the coast of South America, discovering the estuaries of the Orinoco and Rio de la Plata. His main achievement was to ascertain that Columbus had, in fact, discovered a 'New World', and not Asia, as Columbus himself had maintained.

Over 20 years later, another Florentine navigator, GIOVANNI DA VERRAZZANO (1485-1528), searching for the legendary North-West Passage, sailed through the narrows that now bear his name, and discovered New York Harbour.

A NEW ROLE

Under the rule of the grand dukes of Tuscany (Medicis until 1743, then Hapsburgs up to 1859), Florence sank into a torpor which lasted for over three centuries. Anna Maria Ludovica, last of the Medici line, made a grand final gesture worthy of her Renaissance forebears. Far-sightedly, she bequeathed the entire Medici art collection to the city 'to attract foreigners', on condition that none of it ever be sold or removed from Florence. Her wish was granted, for the foreigners came, a small but steady trickle of privileged young gentlemen doing 'the Grand Tour' of Europe – the traditional finishing touch to a gentleman's education.

In the 19th century, a new breed of traveller appeared – the 'Italianate Englishman', led by the poets Byron and Shelley, and followed by the Brownings, John Ruskin and the Pre-Raphaelites. Rapturous Britons, smitten by the romantic image of Italy, toured or settled in droves, bringing in their wake French, German and Russian tourists. Queen Victoria herself visited the city. Florence Nightingale – named after the city – was born there (there is a statue of her in Santa Croce cloister).

After the dramatic events of the Risorgimento, when the occupying Austrians were expelled, Florence had a brief moment of glory as the capital of the newly unified kingdom of Italy (1865-71). With the transfer of the capital to Rome, the story of Florence merges into Italian history.

THE 20TH CENTURY

Despite the excitement at the time of unification, democracy failed to become firmly established. Crisis followed crisis, and the people lost confidence in the government. During World War I, Italy fought against Germany and Austria, but afterwards felt she had been insufficiently rewarded for her sacrifices. Benito Mussolini's Fascists seized power in 1922 as parliamentary democracy disintegrated.

With the Rome-Berlin Axis of 1937, Mussolini linked the fate of Italy to that of Hitler's Germany, dragging his country into defeat in World War II. The Fascist government fell in 1943, and some of the most heroic battles of the Italian resistance were fought in and around Florence. The retreating Germans blew up all the bridges over the Arno except for the Ponte Vecchio, spared because of its famous past. The city's unique art treasures survived unscathed.

Present-day Florence is an important business centre and university town, as well as a major tourist destination, and its suburbs boast a versatile array of automobile, textiles and manufacturing, industries.

Conscious of their position as the inheritors of a great creative and artistic tradition, the heirs of the Medici are striving to keep their city at the forefront of the world of art, literature and fashion.

The Ponte Vecchio has survived countless floods and the bombs of World War II.

What to See

The big question facing first-time visitors to Florence is 'What should I see first?'. It's all too easy to be intimidated by the sheer quantity of art and architecture in the city – there are nearly 70 museums and art galleries, and 24 historic churches, almost all of them worth visiting. The answer is to accept that you can't see everything, and to concentrate on a few of the more important sights. Our 'Highlights' box (opposite) lists the major attractions, enough to keep you busy for two days at least (three or four if you include the day trips to Pisa and Siena).

For those with more time to spare, we've divided the city into four walking tours, each of which can be covered in a day (though not, of course, if you spend a whole morning or afternoon in one of the art galleries). The same advice applies when visiting the big galleries like the Uffizi and the Palatina – don't try to see everything. Pick out a handful of pictures that appeal to you and spend some time studying them, rather than rushing and trying to take in the entire collection in one go.

Many churches in Florence have coin-operated machines which offer a recorded commentary on the history of the church, and a description of the works of art they contain. There are also coin-operated floodlights to illuminate frescoes that are poorly lit. If you want to use these, take along plenty of small change. Keep in mind, too, that these are places of worship; dress respectably, keep noise to a minimum, and don't intrude if a service is taking place.

The Duomo to the Ponte Vecchio

The historic heart of Florence is a grid of narrow streets between the Duomo (cathedral) and the River Arno. Most of the city's famous sights lie in this area, and can be visited in the course of a day's walk.

FLORENCE HIGHLIGHTS

Piazza del Duomo: Florence's cathedral square, dominated by Brunelleschi's famous cupola atop the impressive Duomo, also includes Giotto's Campanile and Ghiberti's gilded bronze 'gates of Paradise' (Battistero). Duomo open 8.30am-5pm. Free. (See p.24.)

Museo Nazionale del Bargello, *Via del Proconsolo, 4*. Florentine Renaissance sculpture, including works by Michelangelo, Donatello, Giambologna and della Robbia. Open 9am-2pm (1pm on holidays); closed Monday. L8,000. (See p.28.)

Galleria degli Uffizi, *Loggiato degli Uffizi, 6*. 13th-18th century Italian and European art in one of the world's most important and prestigious galleries. Open 9am-7pm (1pm on holidays); closed Monday. L12,000. (See p.38.)

Palazzo Vecchio, *Piazza della Signoria*. Sumptuously decorated medieval palace. Open 9am-7pm (8am-1pm on holidays); closed Thursday. L8,000. (See p.32.)

Ponte Vecchio: medieval bridge (1345), lined with goldsmiths' shops, which has survived floods and wars. (See p.42.)

Palazzo Pitti: majestic 15th-century palace housing the Galleria Palatina, with its magnificently decorated 17th-century rooms and superb collection of 16th-century art. Open 9am-2pm (1pm on holidays); closed Monday. L12,000. (See p.63.)

Basilica di San Miniato al Monte, *Via Monte alle Croci*. One of Italy's most beautiful churches, offering panoramic views over the city. Open 8am-noon and 2-7pm (6pm in winter), 2.30-5.30pm Sunday. Free. (See p.74.)

Pisa: an easy day trip from Florence to see the famous Leaning Tower (closed for restoration at the time of writing) and the neighbouring Gothic cathedral and baptistery. Cathedral open 7.45am-12.45pm and 3-7pm (5pm winter), free. Baptistery open 8am-8pm (summer), 9am-5pm (winter). L5,000. (See p.80.)

Siena: Florence's historical rival, the walled city of Siena, is a wonderful Gothic masterpiece perched high on three hills. The Piazza del Campo is the scene of the famous, twice-yearly Palio bareback horse-race. (See p.82.)

A climb up 463 steps leads to the viewing terrace at the top of Brunelleschi's graceful dome.

PIAZZA DEL DUOMO/ PIAZZA SAN GIOVANNI

A short stroll from Santa Maria Novella railway station will bring you to Piazza San Giovanni, where you get your first, very impressive sight of Florentine religious architecture, with the huge façade of the **Duomo** rising majestically above the pointed roof of the Baptistery (see p.26).

Officially known as Santa Maria del Fiore (Our Lady of the Flower), the Duomo was designed by the great architect Arnolfo di Cambio, and was intended by the proud Florentines as the cathedral which would surpass all the great buildings of antiquity in size and splendour – the space within its green, white and pink marble-faced walls can hold over 20,000 people.

Work began around 1296 on the site of a far smaller 5th-century church, but was not completed until the second half of the 15th century. Its elaborate, Neo-Gothic façade was added in the 19th century. Like most Tuscan churches of the time, the Duomo presents a uniquely local version of Gothic-style architecture, not easily compared to English or French ecclesiastical buildings of the same period.

The mighty **cupola** was the contribution of Filippo Brunelleschi (1377-1446; see p.40), unquestionably the greatest of all the Renaissance architects. The artist had marvelled at the dome on Rome's Pantheon, rebuilt for Emperor Hadrian about AD 125, which was unsurpassed by any other engineering feat.

The ambitious Florentines decided that their showpiece cathedral must have a great dome. In a public competition held in 1418, Brunelleschi submitted the winning design and, just as importantly, a workable building scheme. (The original wooden model of the dome is in the Museo dell'Opera di Santa Maria del Fiore; see p.28.) In Florence, where beauty and art were never the preserve of the rich alone, these competitions used to cause immense popular excitement. Citizens rich and poor, high and low, often sat together as adjudicators.

Brunelleschi's truly magnificent dome, finally completed in 1436 – the first giant cupola since antiquity – was visible for miles, dwarfing the red-tiled rooftops around it, and confirming the feeling of the day that nothing was beyond the science and ingenuity of Renaissance Man. Its diameter of 42m (138ft) is greater than that of the Pantheon, St Peter's in Rome, and St Paul's in London. You can climb up to the top of the lantern and enjoy breathtaking panoramic views over the city.

Most of the Duomo's original statuary was long ago removed to the Museo dell'Opera di Santa Maria del Fiore (see p.28). There are nevertheless some important works of art to be seen in the cathedral. Make sure you take a look at Lorenzo Ghiberti's bronze shrine, below the high altar, which was made to house the remains of St Zenobius (one of Florence's first bishops). The stained-glass rose windows of the Duomo were also designed by the versatile Ghiberti.

Left of the entrance are some rather unusual *trompe l'œil* frescoed 'monuments' to two 15th-century *condottieri*, or mercenary captains, who fought for Florence. The right-hand one, painted by that great master of perspective, Paolo Uccello, commemorates an Englishman, John Hawkwood, the only foreigner ever buried in the Duomo.

If you're lucky enough to be at the Duomo on Easter Sunday, you can witness the famous, centuries-old ceremony of *Scoppio del Carro* (Explosion of the Cart), with its traditional costumes and pageantry. A decorated cart piled high with fireworks is drawn into the piazza by white oxen, and ignited by a model dove which whizzes along a wire from the high altar, signifying the descent of the Holy Spirit.

The Duomo's free-standing **Campanile** (bell-tower) is one of Florence's most graceful landmarks. It was begun in 1334 by that multi-talented genius Giotto, and completed by his successor, Andrea Pisano, in 1359. Pisano actually doubled the thickness of the campanile walls – had he not done so, it would almost certainly have collapsed long ago.

Faced in green, white and pink marble to match the Duomo, the lowest storey bears reliefs designed by Giotto illustrating the Creation of Man, and the *Arti* (trades) and Industries of Florence, while the niches in the second storey contain statues of the Prophets and Sibyls, some of them by Donatello. It's worth making the 414-step climb to the top for an unusual bird's-eye view of the cathedral and city.

Opposite the Duomo lies **Il Battistero** (The Baptistery). Acclaimed as the oldest building in Florence, this precious gem of Romanesque architecture was built in the early 12th century on the site of a Roman temple of Mars, and served for a time as Florence's cathedral. Salvaged Roman columns were used as construction material, and the exterior appearance remains as it was in the time of Dante. Byzantine-style, 13th-century mosaics inside the cupola include scenes from the *Creation*, *Life of St John* and a *Last Judgement*.

The Baptistery's principal claim to fame is its three sets of gilded bronze doors. Those on the south side date from the 14th century and are by Andrea Pisano, while those on the north and east sides were made by Lorenzo Ghiberti in the first half of the 15th century.

A competition to design the north and east doors was held in 1401, financed by one of the richest merchant guilds. Brunelleschi was among those who submitted an entry, but Ghiberti's design was unanimously declared the winner. The two sculptors' entries are exhibited in the Bargello (see p.31), so you can judge their relative merits for yourself.

The east doors, facing the Duomo, were described by an admiring Michelangelo as being fit to be the **'Gates of Paradise'**. The name has stuck ever since. Among the ten panels illustrating Old Testament scenes are numerous sculpted heads and figures; Ghiberti's own self-portrait is on the left-hand door, to the right of the second panel up from the bottom. (The doors are actually copies – the original panels have been restored and are now on display in the Museo dell'Opera di Santa Maria del Fiore; see p.28.)

The stone column standing on its own behind the Baptistery commemorates a tree that burst into bloom when the remains of the revered Florentine bishop, Saint Zenobius, were carried past one wintry day, many centuries ago.

One of ten carved panels adorning the 'Gates of Paradise' – 'Joseph sold to the Merchants'.

On the corner of Via dei Calzaiuoli, south of the Baptistery, is the graceful 14th-century **Loggia del Bigallo**, once part of the headquarters of a society for the care of orphans. Across the street lies the headquarters of one of Florence's oldest and most respected social institutions, the Brotherhood of the Misericordia. The unpaid volunteers, easily recognized in their black hooded capes, work on rotating shifts around the clock to provide free assistance to the poor and needy, and also run Florence's emergency ambulance service. This remarkable democratic institution was established 600 years before the existence of the Red Cross or Social Security.

The **Museo dell'Opera di Santa Maria del Fiore** is the Duomo's own museum (entrance across the street at the east end of the Duomo), where many of its most precious treasures and original sculptures have been taken for safekeeping. Highlights include a sumptuous 14th-15th-century, silver-faced altar from the Baptistery; rich gold and silver reliquaries (one of which houses the index finger of Saint John, Florence's patron saint); Brunelleschi's original wooden model of the Duomo's cupola; Donatello's harrowing wooden effigy of Mary Magdalen; and two beautiful sculptured choir lofts (*cantoria*), one by Donatello, and the other by Luca della Robbia. Here, too, is housed Michelangelo's unfinished *Pietà*; it is said that he intended it for his own tomb.

Via dell' Oriuolo, at the right-hand corner of Piazza del Duomo, leads to the **Museo 'Firenze com'era'** ('Florence as it was'), where you will find a great number of paintings, prints and photographs illustrating the city's physical history. This museum was formerly a monastery.

From the same corner, the narrow alleyway of Via del Proconsolo leads southward to the forbidding, battlemented fortress of the Palazzo del Bargello, which houses the **Museo Nazionale del Bargello**. Florence's original town hall, and one of its earliest public buildings (begun about 1250), the Bargello served as the seat of the magistrates (*podestà*) responsible for law and order, and later housed the Captain of Justice (*bargello*), the 16th-century equivalent of today's police commissioner.

Criminals were imprisoned, tortured and executed here, and the outer walls were decorated with lifelike images of traitors and murderers hung by the neck, or by one foot – horrific warnings to would-be wrongdoers. The grisly frescoes were often commissioned from the city's best artists – Botticelli himself painted the Pazzi Conspirators in 1478.

The Bargello is to sculpture what the Uffizi is to painting, for it houses many Renaissance masterpieces. The first

Verrochio's 'David with the head of Goliath' stands with other masterpieces in the Bargello.

Frescoes from the school of Giotto decorate the walls of the Bargello chapel.

room beyond the entrance is the **Sala Michelangelo** (Hall of Michelangelo) – note the wall marks 3m (9ft) above the floor, recording the water level of the 1966 flood.

Michelangelo was only 21 when he finished his early masterpiece, *The Drunken Bacchus*, beautifully god-like but perhaps a little unsteady on his legs! He sculpted the marble *Pitti Tondo* of the Virgin and Child eight years later in 1504, while also working on his famous *David*. For a portrait of the artist, see Daniele da Volterra's bronze bust of Michelangelo at his sourest. Also on display here are two colossal marble statues of Adam and Eve by Bandinelli; *Mercury*, Giambologna's remarkable bronze; Cellini's handsome bronze bust of Cosimo I de' Medici, and the small bronze model for his *Perseus* in the Loggia dei Lanzi.

A door leads into the attractive courtyard, softened by the brownish hues of its *pietra forte*, and covered with stone plaques bearing the arms of successive *podestà*. A 14th-century stone staircase leads to an arcaded loggia on the first floor, where you'll see Giambologna's series of remarkably lifelike bronze birds surrounding a marble figure representing Architecture. The birds served as garden or fountain decorations for one of the Medici villas.

The first floor exhibits range from Italian and Tuscan ceramics and old Murano glass to French Limoges enamels and astonishing engraved seashells. The 14th-century chapel contains frescoes painted by a pupil of Giotto, while the sharp-featured man behind the kneeling figure on the right is said to be Dante.

If you are pushed for time, head straight for the **Great Hall**, whose works capture the spirit of early Renaissance Florence. Donatello's movingly human *St George* (1416) dominates the back wall of this high-vaulted room. Commissioned by the armourers' guild as their contribution to the exterior decorations of Orsanmichele (see p.43), its depth and sense of movement are generally held to represent the first great sculptural achievement of the Renaissance.

Donatello's bronze *David*, the first free-standing nude statue of the Renaissance, once graced the courtyard of the Medici palace. In contrast to the 'modern' feeling of *Saint George,* the *David* has an antique sensuality about it, while the delightful bronze *Amore* (cupid) is positively Roman in style. More personal and dramatic are the two marble versions of *St John the Baptist.*

Be sure to take a look at Ghiberti's and Brunelleschi's original bronze panels (*The Sacrifice of Abraham*) for the Baptistery design competition of 1401 (see p.27) – clearly, it was a close contest; they're on the right wall towards the back of the room.

The Sala di Verrocchio on the second floor has Verrocchio's bronze *David* (c.1471), which is said to have been modelled on the sculptor's 19-year-old pupil, the illustrious Leonardo da Vinci.

Across the street from the Bargello is the church known as the **Badia Fiorentina**, with its graceful bell-tower, part Romanesque, part Gothic. Go inside for a moment to admire Filippino Lippi's delightful *Madonna Appearing to Saint Bernard*; you will find it on the left of the church as you enter.

PIAZZA DELLA SIGNORIA

Continue through the small Piazza San Firenze and turn right into Via dei Gondi, which leads to the wide expanse of the **Piazza della Signoria**.

If the Piazza del Duomo is the religious heart of Florence, this is its political counterpart. The city rulers have gathered here since the 13th century, and the present-day offices of the city council are still housed in the Palazzo Vecchio. In summer the square is crowded with tourists, visiting the Palazzo and the neighbouring Uffizi, admiring the wealth of statuary, enjoying a drink in the open-air cafés, and having their picture taken amid the tame Florentine pigeons.

Dominating the square is the fortress-like **Palazzo Vecchio**, which is also known as the Palazzo della Signoria, after the highest tier of the city's 15th-century Republican government, known as the *Signoria*, who met here. Designed by Arnolfo di Cambio, the architect who designed the Duomo, and intended to house the city's government, it acquired the name *Palazzo Vecchio* (Old Palace) after 1549, when the Medici moved their headquarters across the river to the Palazzo Pitti (see p.63). Its foundations were laid in 1299, as part of a mammoth public building programme.

The palazzo's off-centred 94m (308ft) tower, added in 1310, helps to soften the building's squareness, and complements its own off-centre position on the piazza. There's a practical, if unusual reason for this. The area around the 16th-century Neptune Fountain was formerly the site of the Uberti family's palazzo. One of Florence's leading 13th-century aristocratic Ghibelline families, and one of the most hated, the Uberti were expelled *en masse* from the city, their palace razed to the ground, and its site cursed for all eternity. The Palazzo della Signoria was laid out to avoid this tainted land.

The ornate courtyard of the palazzo comes as a surprise after the medieval austerity of the exterior. This was part of a 16th-century scheme by Vasari to brighten up the palace following the marriage of Cosimo I's son to an Austrian princess (the frescoes are of Austrian cities). Verrocchio's bronze *putto* (cherub) fountain was specially brought from Lorenzo de' Medici's villa at Careggi, as a final touch (the original is inside).

The palazzo's highlights include the massive **Salone dei Cinquecento** on the first floor. Built to house the parliament of the short-lived Florentine republic declared in 1494 (see p.16), it was turned into a grand throne room by Cosimo I, decorated with giant Vasari frescoes of Florentine victories, and Michelangelo's statue of *Victory* representing Cosimo's triumph over Siena in 1554-55. Three centuries later, the first parliament of a united Italy met here.

A small door to the right of the main entrance allows visitors to peek into the **Studiolo di Francesco I**, a little gem of a study designed by Vasari. It is covered from floor to barrel-vaulted ceiling with painted allegorical panels (representing Fire, Water, Earth and Air), and two Bronzino portraits of Cosimo I and his consort gazing down haughtily.

Across the hall, another door leads into the **Quartiere di Leone X**, the apartments of Leo X (the first Medici pope).

Feeding pigeons is always a popular pastime for tourists gathered in the Piazza della Signoria.

The Palazzo Vecchio has been home to the city council since the 14th century.

The rooms are sumptuously decorated with frescoes celebrating the heroic achievements of the Medici family. Stairs lead up to the equally sumptuous **Quartiere degli Elementi** on the second floor, with painted allegories on the theme of the elements. The Terraza di Saturno at the back provides a fine view across the river to San Miniato and the Forte di Belvedere.

A dizzying gallery above the Salone connects with the **Quartiere di Eleonora** (the apartments of Eleonora of Toledo, Cosimo I's wife), a riot of gilt, painted ceilings and rich furnishings. Note the fine frescoes by Bronzino in Eleonora's private chapel.

The splendid 15th-century **Sala dei Gigli** (Hall of the Lilies), all blue and gold, is lavishly decorated with Florentine heraldry, a gilt-panelled ceiling, bright Ghirlandaio frescoes, and superb doors inlaid with figures of Dante and Petrarch. Here stands Donatello's original bronze of *Judith and Holofernes* – a copy of it is in the piazza outside.

The adjoining Cancelleria was used as an office by Machiavelli, and now houses a lifelike, coloured bust and portrait of the author of *The Prince*. Next door is the splendid **Guardaroba**, a cupboard-lined room whose wooden panels were painted with maps

by two learned Dominican friars (1563-87). The 57 maps illustrate the extent of the world known to Western civilization in the late 16th century.

To the right of the palace is the **Loggia della Signoria**, or Loggia dei Lanzi, built in the late 14th century. Originally a covered vantage point for city officials at public ceremonies, it took its later name from Cosimo I's Swiss-Germano *Landsknechts* (Italianized to *Lanzichenecchi*), his mercenary bodyguards, who used it as a guard-room during his nine-year residence in the palazzo. Since the late 18th century it has been used as an open-air museum of sculpture.

The first of its celebrated works, Cellini's fine bronze *Perseus*, was lodged here on Cosimo's order in the early 1550s. The two Giambologna works (*Rape of the Sabines* and *Hercules and the Centaur*) were added towards the end of the century, while the Roman statues at the back were 18th-century Medici donations.

Cellini's *Perseus*, a masterpiece of bronze-casting, came within an inch of disaster during the casting process. The sculptor himself, in his lively autobiography, describes the agonizing moment when he had to throw all his pewter vessels – over 200 plates, goblets and pots – into the molten metal in order to keep it pouring smoothly into the mould. The little figures embellishing the statue's base might not have been there today if Eleonora of Toledo, Cosimo's wife, had had her way. Wanting the statuettes for herself, she kept badgering Cellini to give them to her; but he, with an eye to public acclaim, ensured their destiny by soldering them firmly onto the base. These are actually copies; the originals are now in the Bargello.

All this statuary was part of Cosimo's ambitious scheme to decorate the piazza, which included the bronze equestrian statue of himself by Giambologna, and the massive Neptune Fountain designed by Ammannati. He even toyed with a typically grandiose suggestion of Michelangelo's to extend the Loggia dei Lanzi all the way round the piazza.

The raised stone platform running the length of the palazzo's façade was used as a platform for speakers to address crowds in the square (called the *arringhiera,* from which came the English word 'harangue'), and provided a public showcase for Florentine sculpture. A bronze *marzocco* – a heraldic lion bearing the city's arms (the symbol of Florence) – has graced the piazza for almost as long as the palazzo itself (what you see today is a copy; the original is in the Bargello). Donatello's stunning bronze of *Judith and Holofernes* was transferred here from the Medici Palace in 1494 (a copy; the original is preserved within the palace). Michelangelo's *David* was positioned here in 1504 as a Republican symbol. Sculpted in just two years from a giant block of marble on which an earlier artist had made a clumsily unsuccessful start, *David* was eventually moved to the Accademia (see p.50) in 1873 and replaced by a copy. The present version is a second copy commissioned during this century. The rather grotesque statue of *Hercules and Cacus* beside it is the work of a 16th-century sculptor, Bandinelli. He was also responsible for, among other things, the seated statue of Cosimo I's father in Piazza San Lorenzo.

Between the Palazzo Vecchio and the Arno, the Uffizi Gallery stretches down either side of the narrow, colonnaded Piazzale degli Uffizi. Built by Vasari in the second half of the 16th century, the building was

CHURCHES, PALACES, MUSEUMS AND GALLERIES

(See also the list of Florence Highlights on p.23)

BASILICA DI SANTA CROCE, *Piazza Santa Croce.* Giotto frescoes, Donatello's crucifix, tombs of Michelangelo, Machiavelli, Galileo. Open 8am-12.30pm and 3-6pm (3-5.30pm Sunday). Free. (See p.59.)

BASILICA DI SAN LORENZO, *Piazza San Lorenzo.* Works by Donatello and Filipo Lippi, Michelangelo's *Biblioteca Laurenziana.* Open 8am-noon and 3.30-5.30pm (Sunday afternoons only). Free. (See p.44.)

BATTISTERO, *Piazza San Giovanni.* 13th-century mosaics and Ghiberti's bronze doors. 1.30-6pm (9am-1pm on holidays). Free. (See p.26.)

CAMPANILE DI GIOTTO, *Piazza del Duomo.* Giotto's fine bell tower for the Duomo. Open 8.30am-7pm (9am-4.30pm, 1 November-31 March). L5,000. (See p.26.)

CAPPELLE MEDICÉE, *Piazza Madonna degli Aldobrandini.* Tombs of the Medici rulers; Michelangelo sculptures in the New Sacristy. Open 9am-2pm (1pm on holidays); closed Monday. L9,000. (See p.46.)

DUOMO (CATTEDRALE DI SANTA MARIA DEL FIORE), *Piazza del Duomo.* Brunelleschi's famous cupola. Open 10am-5pm. Free. (See p.24.)

GALLERIA DELL'ACCADEMIA, *Via Ricasoli, 60.* Michelangelo's *David* and several unfinished sculptures, as well as Florentine art. Open 9am-7pm (2pm on Sundays); closed Monday. L12,000. (See p.50.)

MUSEO ARCHEOLOGICO, *Via della Colonna, 36.* Egyptian, Etruscan and Greek art. Open 9am-2pm; closed Monday. L8,000. (See p.52.)

MUSEO DELL'OPERA DI SANTA CROCE, *Piazza Santa Croce, 16.* Cloisters, Pazzi Chapel, sculpture and artwork from Santa Croce church. Open 10am-12.30pm and 2.30-6.30pm (summer); 10am-12.30pm and 3-5pm (1 October-28 February). L3,000. (See p.60.)

MUSEO DELL'OPERA DI SANTA MARIA DEL FIORE, *Piazza del Duomo, 9.* Sculpture and religious art from the Duomo. Open 9am-7.30pm (6pm in winter); closed Sunday. L5,000. (See p.28.)

MUSEO DI SAN MARCO, *Piazza San Marco, 1.* Restored monastery housing the religious paintings of Fra Angelico. Open 9am-2pm (1pm on holidays); closed Monday. L8,000. (See p.49.)

MUSEO STORICO TOPOGRAFICO 'FIRENZE COM'ERA', *Via dell'Oriuolo, 4.* The history of the Florentine city, 'as it was'. Open 9am-2pm (8am-1pm on holidays); closed Thursday. L3,000. (See p.28.)

intended to house the headquarters of the various government offices (*uffizi* is Italian for 'offices'), the official mint, and workshops for Medici craftsmen. It is now the home of one of the world's most famous art galleries.

THE UFFIZI

Ideally, the best way to get to grips with the abundant treasures of the Uffizi is to tackle one room a day. Unfortunately, this would take almost 40 days, and most tourists have only a morning or even less to spare. If you want to avoid the worst of the crowds, try to come in the late afternoon or early evening, after most of the coach parties have left.

Exhibited in chronological order, the paintings comprise the cream of Italian and European art from the 13th to 18th centuries. Begun by Cosimo I and added to by his successors, the collection was then bequeathed to the people of Florence in 1737 by Anna Maria Ludovica, the last of the Medici dynasty (see pp.11 and 20), on condition that it never leaves the city. To avoid being overwhelmed by the sheer quantity of art, you should feel absolutely no qualms about skipping some of the 37 or so rooms that lead off the two first-floor galleries. We have listed the highlights below.

(At the time of writing, the west wing of the Uffizi, damaged by a terrorist bomb in May 1993, was closed for repairs. The most popular works from that section, including Michelangelo's *Doni Tondo*, Raphael's *Madonna with a Goldfinch*, and Caravaggio's *Young Bacchus*, are being displayed in the former church of San Piero Scherragio, an 11th-century building incorporated into the ground floor of the Uffizi beyond the ticket office.)

The first rooms contain those early Tuscan greats, Cimabue and Giotto. In their altarpieces depicting enthroned Madonnas (painted in the years 1280 and 1310 respectively), the mosaic-like stiffness of Cimabue's work contrasts vividly with Giotto's innovative depth and more expressive figures.

The greatest painter of the 14th-century Sienese school was Simone Martini – see his graceful *Annunciation* (1333), painted for Siena's cathedral. Of the later Italian Gothic masterpieces, Gentile da Fabriano's *Adoration of the Magi* (1423) is the most exquisite.

The Florentine School of the early 15th century produced Masaccio's *Madonna and Child with St Anne* (c.1424), an early Renaissance breakthrough because of its new 'realism'; Fra Angelico's *Coronation of the Virgin*, full of light and music; and Paolo Uccello's *Battle of San Romano* (1456), an astounding exercise in perspective and the use of space. Originally consisting of three panels (the others are in Paris and London), it once hung in the bedroom of Lorenzo Il Magnifico. See also Piero della Francesca's powerful portrait of the *Duke of Urbino* (1465), warts and all!

Among the best loved and most reproduced of Renaissance paintings are Botticelli's haunting *Primavera* (Spring; 1477-78) and his renowned *Birth of Venus* (c.1485). Venus is said to be modelled on 'La Bella Simonetta Vespucci', mistress of the luckless Giuliano de' Medici. Botticelli's lifelike but theatrical *Adoration of the Magi* features portraits of the Medici family – Cosimo Il Vecchio, his son Piero Il Gottoso, and grandsons Lorenzo Il Magnifico and Giuliano (smugly standing on the extreme left, a few years before his murder). Botticelli himself, in a yellow cloak, gazes out on the far right.

One entire room is devoted to Leonardo da Vinci. The *Baptism of Christ* (c.1474-75) was mostly the work of his great teacher, Verrocchio. Although only the background and the angel on the left were the work of the 18-year-old Leonardo, when Verrocchio saw how exquisitely his pupil had rendered the angel, he swore never to touch a paintbrush again. The *Annunciation* (c.1472-77) is entirely Leonardo's work, as is the *Adoration of the Magi* (1481). The latter is not just unfinished, but barely begun, merely sketched out in preparatory *chiaroscuro*, or light and shade, but this is sufficient to show Leonardo's unique approach to the subject. (It has been suggested that the young man looking out of the picture on the right-hand edge is in fact a self-portrait.)

The Great Names of Florentine Art

GIOVANNI CIMABUE (1240-1302) moved away from the Byzantine tradition to found the Florentine school of **painting**, but it was the naturalism of GIOTTO (1266-1337) that made Florence into the first city of Italian art.

The Early Renaissance was ushered in by MASACCIO (1401-28), with his solid modelled human figures, followed by ANDREA DEL CASTAGNO (1423-57); PAOLO UCCELLO (1397-1475), master of perspective; and the melancholic FILIPPO LIPPI (1406-69). In the realm of religious art, the outstanding painters were FRA ANGELICO (1387-1455), noted for his purity of line and colour; ANDREA VERROCCHIO (1435-88), Leonardo da Vinci's teacher and a fine sculptor; DOMENICO GHIRLANDAIO (1449-94), famous for his frescoes; the exquisitely lyrical BOTTICELLI (1444-1510); and FILIPPINO LIPPI (1457-1504), son of Filippo.

Art reached new heights in the early 16th century with the works of artist and scientist LEONARDO DA VINCI (1452-1519), as well as those of MICHELANGELO (1475-1564) – sculptor, architect, painter and poet – and RAPHAEL (1483-1520), who has come to epitomize the period known as the High Renaissance.

The great names of Florentine **architecture** were GIOTTO, BRUNELLESCHI (1377-1446), ALBERTI (1404-72) and MICHELOZZO (1396-1472). The leading **sculptors** were LORENZO GHIBERTI (1378-1455), creator of the famous bronze doors on the Baptistery; DONATELLO (1386-1466), perhaps the greatest Early Renaissance sculptor; LUCA DELLA ROBBIA (1400-82), who specialized in brightly coloured, glazed terracottas; and BENVENUTO CELLINI (1500-71), who also excelled as a goldsmith.

Outstanding among the 15th-century Flemish paintings is Hugo Van der Goes' huge triptych, *Adoration of the Shepherds* (1478), which was painted for the Medici's Flemish agent, Tommaso Portinari. The Portinari family is immortalized on its side-panels. In a sunnier, lighter vein is Ghirlandaio's *Adoration* (1487).

The octagonal room known as the Tribuna, commissioned by the Medici from Buontalenti, symbolizes the four elements; its cupola is encrusted with mother-of-pearl, representing water. The sumptuous 17th-century, inlaid stone table, specially made for the room, took 16 years to complete. Here also are Bronzino's portraits of Cosimo I's Spanish wife, *Eleonora of Toledo*, and their chubby, smiling baby son, Giovanni – one of the most endearing child portraits ever painted.

The *Medici Venus*, a marble nude excavated at Hadrian's Tivoli villa, is thought to be a copy of a 4th-century BC Greek original by Praxiteles. Said to represent Phryne, the notorious Athenian courtesan who became rich through her many lovers, it was apparently Thomas Jefferson's favourite piece of sculpture, for he kept a copy of it in his study.

Among the German masterpieces in the Uffizi, look out for Dürer's *Portrait of His Father* (1490) and *Adoration of the Magi* (1504), and Cranach's lifelike little portraits of *Luther*, his renegade wife, and a solid *Adam and Eve* (1526).

Among the works of the 15th-century Venetian School are Bellini's strange, dreamlike *Sacred Allegory*, painted about 1490; its allegorical significance, however, has never been satisfactorily explained.

The Uffizi contains just one work by the great Michelangelo – his only finished oil painting, a round panel showing the Holy Family, known as the *Doni Tondo* (1503-05). Firmly but humanly treated, it is his earliest known painting.

Equally notable are Raphael's maternal *Madonna del Cardellino* (Madonna of the Goldfinch; c.1505) and a wistful self-portrait painted in

Florence when he was only 23. The works by Titian includes *Flora* (c.1515) and his celebrated, voluptuous nude, the *Venus of Urbino* (1538).

The final few rooms contain Rubens' *Portrait of his Wife*, so glowingly alive it's sad to think she died a year later; Caravaggio's splendidly decadent *Young Bacchus* (1589); and Rembrandt's famous *Portrait of an Old Rabbi*, as well as two self-portraits.

At the far end of the West Corridor is a café with a terrace, which sits above the Loggia dei Lanzi. Here you can sip a glass of freshly squeezed lemonade while enjoying a close-up view of the Palazzo Vecchio's balcony and tower.

PONTE VECCHIO

From the Uffizi exit, walk down to the river and turn right along the embankment. Above the pavement runs the Corridoio Vasariano, a graceful covered walkway built by Vasari in 1565 to link the Uffizi and the Palazzo Vecchio with the Medici's new headquarters in the Palazzo Pitti, so that Grand Duke Cosimo de' Medici could commute between the two without ever getting wet. You can see the Corridoio continuing across the Ponte Vecchio above the shops.

The oldest bridge in Florence, the **Ponte Vecchio**, was the only one to be spared destruction during World War II. The present bridge, complete with shops overhanging the river, dates back to 1345. The sparkling jewellers' and goldsmiths' workshops have been here as long as the bridge, and attract window-shopping tourists. From the terrace in the middle, you can look downstream towards the elegant, softly curved arches of the Ponte Santa Trinita. Blown up by the retreating Germans in August 1944, this bridge was carefully reconstructed, exactly as Ammannati had built it in the 16th century.

The Via Por Santa Maria runs from the Ponte Vecchio back towards the Duomo. One of Florence's busiest shopping streets, it leads to the **Mercato Nuovo** (New Market), housed beneath a 16th-century loggia. The main attraction of the Mercato Nuovo (also known as the Straw Market) is the stalls selling leather goods, baskets, lace and souvenirs. Look for the 17th-century bronze statue of a boar, known as *Il Porcellino* (the little boar), on the south side. Tradition has it that if you stroke his nose and throw a coin into the fountain, you will be sure to return to the city. In the centre of the market is a marble circle, inelegantly called the *Batticulo* (the 'arse-whacker'), where, in the 16th century, swindlers and welchers were soundly beaten.

Turn right one block beyond the market and you will find the unusual church of **Orsanmichele**. The original building was an open-sided loggia, like Mercato Nuovo, built in 1337 for use as a market. When it was converted to a church in 1380, the sides were built with Gothic windows (later bricked up), and the two upper storeys, added in the early 15th century, were used as an emergency granary. In the rear left-hand corner of the ceiling you can actually see the ducts down which grain was poured into waiting sacks. Mystical and mysterious, the pillared interior is dominated by Orcagna's bulky but splendid 14th-century altarpiece, which was built around a miracle-working image of the Madonna.

The goldsmiths on the Ponte Vecchio have attracted admiring window-shoppers for centuries.

Adopted by the city's wealthy merchant and craft guilds, the church's fortress-like, plain, square exterior was embellished with Gothic-style niches and statues during the late 14th and early 15th centuries. Each guild paid for one of the 14 niches and commissioned a statue of its patron or favourite saint.

On the north side of the church stands a copy of Donatello's *Saint George* (the original stands in the Bargello). Commissioned by the armourers' guild, this work was one of the first masterpieces of Renaissance sculpture.

Ghiberti's statues of *Saint Matthew* and *Saint Stephen* can be seen on the west side of the building, opposite the 13th-century Palazzo dell'Arte della Lana. Look at the impressive upper floors (*Saloni*), reached via an overhead walkway from the palazzo; they were once the headquarters of the powerful wool-merchants' guild. The views alone are definitely well worth the climb.

On the east side runs Via dei Calzaiuoli, another busy shopping street, lined with numerous ice-cream shops and pizza bars, and leading back to the Piazza del Duomo.

San Lorenzo to Santissima Annunziata

SAN LORENZO

Across the street from the Baptistery, the narrow Borgo San Lorenzo leads into a small square below the church of **San Lorenzo**. The rough, unfaced stone façade of this church looks for all the world like a huge Tuscan barn. Built by Brunelleschi in 1425-46, it was supposed to have been completed by Michelangelo but never was, and for once, 19th-century architects didn't try to finish the job.

Florence's first entirely Renaissance church and one of Filippo Brunelleschi's earliest architectural triumphs, the building was begun on the site of a 4th-century basilica, and completed with a substantial injection of cash from the Medicis. Cosimo Il Vecchio then had his palace built within sight of the church.

The horizontal perspective of the uncluttered interior is a

striking example – in an age of soaring Gothic – of new and exciting effects achieved with the simplest means. Note the purity and elegance of the grey, classical *pietra serena* columns. The Medici family arms adorn the ceiling.

A door in the left wall of the church leads to the cloister and the stairs up to the **Biblioteca Laurenziana** (Laurentian Library), one of Michelangelo's architectural masterpieces. A monumental staircase climbs to the tranquil reading room, graced with a splendid wooden ceiling and earthy terracotta floor. Commissioned by Pope Clement VII in 1524 to house a precious collection of Medici books and manuscripts, and opened to the public in 1571, it's regarded by many as one of the most beautiful libraries in the world.

The peaceful cloisters of San Lorenzo are overlooked by the Laurentian Library.

Lorenzo de Medici's tomb in the New Sacristy was one of Michelangelo's greatest works.

The sobre church was always closely associated with the Medici family, many of whom are buried here. Cosimo Il Vecchio himself is in the crypt beneath the dome, while his father and mother are in the Old Sacristy, along with his two sons, Piero Il Gottoso and Giovanni, in a sumptuous porphyry and bronze tomb by Verrocchio. That giant of early Renaissance art, Donatello, is buried in the left transept.

To see the most sumptuous of the Medici tombs, you must leave the church and go all around to the far end, where you will find the entrance to the **Cappelle Medicée** (Medici Chapels) in Piazza Madonna degli Aldobrandini. From the crypt, filled with the tombs of minor family members, a staircase leads up to the **Cappella dei Principi** (the Chapel of the Princes). This 17th-century baroque extravaganza was intended by Cosimo I as the family burial vault to surpass all others. The workmanship of multi-coloured inlaid marble and semi-precious stones is astounding – it took three centuries to complete – even if by today's standards the taste is doubtful. Six massive sarcophagi bear the mortal remains of (left to right from the entrance) Cosimo III, Francesco I, Cosimo I, Ferdinando I, Cosimo II and Ferdinando II.

The main attraction here, however, is the **New Sacristy** (*Sagrestia Nuova*), which is reached via a corridor beside the stairs. This is an amazing one-man show by Michelangelo, who spent more than 14 years designing the interior and creating most of the sculptures. Commissioned in 1520 by the future Pope Clement VII (the illegitimate son of Giuliano de' Medici) as a worthy resting-place for both his father and uncle (Lorenzo Il Magnifico), it was also to accommodate two recently deceased cousins (also named Giuliano and Lorenzo).

The two more illustrious members of the Medici clan are buried to the right of the entrance, beneath Michelangelo's fine *Virgin and Child*, which is flanked by figures of the Medici patron saints, Cosmas and Damian. The undistinguished cousins, ironically enough, have been immortalized by Michelangelo in two of the most famous funeral monuments of all time. On the right stands an idealized, warlike Giuliano above two splendid figures symbolizing *Night* and *Day*, reclining on the elegantly curved sarcophagus. The unfinished face of *Day* (on the right), with the visible marks of Michelangelo's chisel, makes the figure all the more remarkable. *Night* is accompanied by the symbols of darkness – an owl, a mask, and the moon upon her brow.

Opposite, a pensive Lorenzo sits above *Dawn* and *Dusk*. The specially foreshortened effect of the upper windows gives the cupola a feeling of still greater height. The walls behind the altar bear architectural sketches and markings, some of which are attributed to Michelangelo himself.

Out in the sunshine of the piazza, you can turn left into the busy, leather-scented street market of Via dell'Ariento, or turn right along Via dei Gori, beneath grim, rusticated walls bristling with medieval iron rings and torch holders.

The walls belong to the **Palazzo Medici-Riccardi** (entrance around the corner on Via Cavour). Built by Michelozzo in the 15th century, it was the home of the Medici until they moved to the Palazzo Vecchio in 1540 (see p.32), and now houses Florence's *Carabinieri-* (police-) guarded Prefecture. Rest for a while in the peaceful little walled garden behind the main courtyard, then climb up to the tiny family **chapel** to see Benozzo Gozzoli's fresco, the *Procession of the Magi*. Painted in 1459, in rich, warm colours, it's a lavish pictorial record of everybody who was anybody in 15th-century Florence, including, of course, the whole Medici clan and their supporters. The chapel remains exactly as the Medici knew it. The ground-floor museum features

The Medici Arms

Students of heraldry will be busy in Florence, for the coats of arms of wealthy families, trade guilds, city wards and justices embellish the façades of many palaces, towers and churches.

The most famous, of course, are the ubiquitous arms of the Medici family, with their six balls, which appear all over Florence. The balls are said to represent pills, for the Medici, whose name means 'doctors', were originally members of the guild of spice merchants and apothecaries. Five balls are coloured red, but the top ball is blue and bears the golden lily of France – a gift from Louis XI of France in the 15th century.

An interesting postscript: the three balls of the traditional pawnbroker's sign evolved from the Medici arms.

Lorenzo's death mask, some family portraits and numerous works of art. Continue along the busy thoroughfare of Via Cavour to the open square of Piazza San Marco.

PIAZZA SAN MARCO

The Dominican church and monastery of San Marco houses one of Florence's most evocative museums: the **Museo di San Marco**. Fra Angelico (1387-1455) lived here as a monk, and most of his finest paintings and frescoes, including the great *Deposition* altarpiece, can be seen in the Pilgrim's Hospice, to the right of the entrance. Across the graceful, columned cloister, with its venerable cedar tree, a corridor behind the convent bell leads to the Small Refectory, decorated with a vivid Ghirlandaio mural of *The Last Supper* – a favourite subject for monastery dining rooms.

The great bell, resting placidly in the cloister, has had a chequered career. Donated by Cosimo de' Medici, it was known as *La Piagnona* (The Great Moaner); Savonarola's puritanical supporters were nicknamed *I Piagnoni* after it, and it was tolled to alert the monks when Savonarola's enemies came to arrest him in 1498 (see p.19). For this act of treason, the bell was spitefully condemned to 50 years of exile outside the city, and was whipped through the streets all the way to its new home.

Upstairs in the dormitory, you can visit the monks' cells, each one bearing a fresco by Fra Angelico or one of his pupils. His famous *Annunciation* is located in cell number 3. At the end of the row to the right of the stairs are the two cells reserved for Cosimo de' Medici's meditations, and at the furthest end of the dormitory, the quarters of Girolamo Savonarola, the monastery's fiery prior and sworn enemy of the Medici. You can see his haunting portrait, painted by fellow monk Fra Bartolomeo; the banner he carried through the streets of Florence; and a painting of his grisly execution by hanging and burning on Piazza della Signoria.

Michelozzo's superb colonnaded library leads off the dormitory. Its light and airy interior displays a number of illuminated choir-books.

From the west side of Piazza San Marco, Via degli Arrazieri leads to a high wall on the left. A wooden door at the far end gives access to the refectory of **Cenacolo di Santa Apollonia** in a former Benedictine nunnery, whose walls are graced by the frescoes of Andrea del Castagno (1423-57). From *The Last Supper* to *The Resurrection*, these frescoes show him to be a master of vigorous forms and colours.

GALLERIA DELL'ACCADEMIA

At the other end of Piazza San Marco is a 14th-century loggia, beneath which is the entrance to the Accademia di Belle Arti (Fine Arts). Founded by Cosimo I in the 16th century, the school was enlarged in 1784, with the addition of an exhibition hall and a collection of Florentine paintings. This is the **Galleria dell'Accademia** (the entrance is along the side street beyond the loggia). Its collection of 13th-16th-century Florentine School paintings is second only to the Uffizi's. There are also tapestries and furniture, including some typical Florentine marriage chests.

The gallery's main attraction is its six sculptures by Michelangelo, including the original *David*, perhaps the most famous piece of sculpture in the Western world. It was brought here from the Piazza della Signoria in 1873 and is displayed in a purpose-built domed room constructed in 1882. Commissioned in 1501 as a symbol of Florence, its balanced and harmonious composition and mastery of technique marked it out as a masterpiece of Renaissance sculpture. The other works are all unfinished, but provide a remarkable illustration of Michelangelo's technique. He claimed that all his sculptures already existed within the block of marble, and that he only had to reveal them. These figures, apparently struggling to emerge from the rough marble, offer a wonderful expression of his philosophy.

PIAZZA DELLA SANTISSIMA ANNUNZIATA

From the Piazza San Marco, a walk along Via C. Battisti leads to the Piazza della Santissima Annunziata, Florence's prettiest square and perhaps the finest example of Renaissance architecture in the city.

The piazza, with graceful colonnades on three sides, was probably designed by Brunelleschi when he built the Spedale degli Innocenti (see p.52) in the early 1440s. The church of **Santissima Annunziata** was added in 1444-81. The architect, Michelozzo, conformed to Brunelleschi's original vision, ensuring the piazza's lasting harmony. The

The Galleria dell'Accademia was founded for the benefit of the city's School of Fine Arts.

two 17th-century fountains and Giambologna's equestrian statue of Grand Duke Ferdinando I add to the feeling of spaciousness of the square.

The church entrance leads into an atrium, decorated with frescoes by Andrea del Sarto and others, from which a large door gives access to the extravagantly decorated interior. Immediately left of the entrance is the 15th-century shrine of the Annunziata. It shelters an old painting of the Annunciation, shown only on special feast days, and said to have been painted by a monk with the help of an angel. The painting is reputed to have miraculous properties, and has been the object of pilgrimages and offerings for centuries.

The unusual circular choir survives from the 15th century, but many of the decorations date from the late 17th century.

The **Galleria dello Spedale degli Innocenti**, on the east side of the square, exhibits 15th- and 16th-century sculptures and paintings belonging to Florence's foundling hospital (*Spedale degli Innocenti*), built to Brunelleschi's design in the 1440s; it was the first foundling hospital in Europe. Note the 15th-century glazed terracotta roundels of swaddled babes by Andrea della Robbia on the arched façade – these are the 'della Robbia babies' that so appealed to Lucy Honeychurch, the heroine of EM Forster's novel, *A Room With A View*. Under the left-hand end of the colonnade is the place where abandoned babies were left.

The archway to the left of the Spedale leads to one of Italy's most important museums, housed in a former grand-ducal palace. The **Museo Archeologico** boasts important collections of ancient Egyptian, Greek and Etruscan art. Among its highlights are the famous, 6th-century BC, Greek François Vase; two remarkable Etruscan bronzes, the *Chimera* (a mythological creature), and the *Arringatore* (the orator); and an impressive collection of painted Greek vases. The superbly reconstructed Etruscan tombs in the gardens were damaged in the 1966 flood.

Santa Maria Novella to Santa Croce

The first view of Florence for travellers emerging from the railway station is the slender campanile of Santa Maria Novella rising across the square. This is only the back view of one of Florence's greatest monastic churches; to appreciate the beauty of its marble façade you must walk round into Piazza Santa Maria Novella.

The church of **Santa Maria Novella** was designed by Dominican architects in the mid-13th century, and a Dominican community still resides within its precincts. The upper part of the bold, inlaid marble front was completed in Renaissance style by the architect Leon Battista Alberti, who was also responsible for the graceful Palazzo Rucellai nearby. (The lower Gothic part is a century older.) One of the few Florentine churches which the Medici didn't pay for, it was funded by the Rucellai family, who had their name put up in large Roman letters under the top cornice, with the family emblem of a billowing sail repeated along the frieze – to make sure their generosity wouldn't go unnoticed.

Walk beneath the soaring vaults of the 100m (328ft) nave to the cluster of richly frescoed family chapels surrounding the altar. The chancel is decorated with frescoes by Ghirlandaio and his pupils showing *Scenes from the Lives of the Virgin and Saint John*, which were paid for by the wealthy Tornabuoni family. Ghirlandaio, Florence's leading 'social' painter of the late 15th century, peopled his frescoes with members of the Tornabuoni clan – one of whom was the mother of Lorenzo Il Magnifico – all dressed in the latest fashions.

To the right of the altar is the Filippo Strozzi Chapel, colourfully frescoed by Filippino Lippi, son of the painter Fra Filippo, and the Bardi Chapel with 14th-century frescoes. The Gondi Chapel to the left of the altar contains a Brunelleschi crucifix (his reply to

Donatello's 'peasant' in Santa Croce; see p.59); on the extreme left is the Strozzi Chapel, with 14th-century frescoes of *The Last Judgement, Heaven* and *Hell* – its benefactors, of course, depicted in Heaven.

The church's most striking work is Masaccio's *Trinity* (c. 1427) on the wall of the left aisle. Famous for its handling of perspective and a convincing illusion of depth, the fresco depicts the crucifixion in a purely Renaissance architectural setting, dramatically breaking away from the established canons of religious art. You'll probably see someone praying or lighting a votive candle in front of it, just as you may hear Mass being said in one of the frescoed chapels. It's all part of the beauty of a city whose life, art and history are inextricably intertwined.

To the left of the church lies part of the surviving monastery. The great 14th-century cloister with its three giant cypresses is a haven of tranquillity after the noisy piazza. From here you can admire the church's graceful 14th-century campanile at close range. Known as the *Chiostro Verde* (green cloister) after the greenish tint of the frescoes once painted here by Paolo Uccello (see p.40), it is flanked by the Refectory (where some detached surviving frescoes are now preserved), a smaller cloister, and the famous **Cappellone degli Spagnoli** (Spanish Chapel), an impressive, vaulted chapter-house named in honour of Cosimo I's Spanish wife, Eleonora of Toledo. Gigantic 14th-century frescoes cover its four walls. The artist incorporated a picture of the Duomo complete with its cupola, 60 years before it was actually completed.

From the far end of the Piazza Santa Maria, the Via dei Fossi leads down to the river (note the stone obelisks, which marked the turning points in the annual 16th-century horseraces). Turn right along Borgo Ognissanti to visit the church of **Ognissanti** (All Saints). Despite its fine 17th-century façade, and the della Robbia glazed terracotta relief over the doorway, the church dates from around 1250. Its builders, the *Umiliati* ('Humble Ones'), were a monastic community who ran a remarkably successful wool business; they are said to have been among the first to put Florence on the road to financial prosperity.

The church contains Botticelli's *Saint Augustine*, and in the refectory, Ghirlandaio's famous *The Last Supper*, both commissioned by the wealthy Vespucci family, several of whose members are buried here, as is Botticelli himself.

From the square in front of the church you can follow the river westwards to the public park known as the **Cascine**, formerly the site of the Medici dairy farms (*cascine*). Its wooded avenues extend for 3km (2 miles) along the riverbank, and contain a fountain dedicated to Shelley, who wrote his *Ode to the West Wind* here.

Alternatively, turn left along the narrow Via della Vigna Nuova towards the town centre, past the elegant façade of the Palazzo Rucellai. Ahead, on the right, you will see the massive, pale gold walls of the **Palazzo Strozzi**, one of the most beautiful private residences in the whole of Florence. Wrought-iron torch holders

The beautiful façade of Santa Maria Novella dates mainly from the 15th century.

and rings for tethering horses are set in the masonry, but the cornice above the street remains unfinished – the money for the works ran out after the death of Filippo Strozzi.

Head right down Via dei Tornabuoni to the Piazza Santa Trinita, with its so-called Column of Justice, a granite pillar taken from the Baths of Caracalla in Rome. It was erected by the Grand Duke Cosimo de' Medici to celebrate his victory over a band of exiled Florentines anxious to overthrow him and re-establish a more democratic government.

On the right side of the piazza is the fine 16th-century façade of the church of **Santa Trinita**. The Gothic interior comes as a complete surprise. It was built between the 13th and 15th centuries on the site of an older church, the remains of which are still visible. Look for the late 15th-century Sassetti Chapel (second on the right from the chancel), with scenes from the life of St Francis by Ghirlandaio. Besides Francesco Sassetti and his family, Lorenzo Il Magnifico and his sons are portrayed in the frescoes against contemporary Florentine backgrounds.

The Strozzi, the Davanzati and the Gianfigliazzi families lived in the area, and sponsored richly frescoed chapels here. So did the Bartolini-Salimbeni family, whose exquisite, early 16th-century palazzo (now the French consulate) faces the church, and the Spini family, whose 13th-century, fortress-like residence (now Palazzo Ferroni) stands at the corner of the piazza.

One of Florence's most unassuming churches, **Santi Apostoli**, hides away on the Piazza del Limbo near Santa Trinita. Legend has it that the church was built by Charlemagne. Inside are some pieces of flint, brought back from Jerusalem's Holy Sepulchre centuries ago by a crusader of the Pazzi family. These are used to light fireworks for the Scoppio del Carro on Easter Sunday (see p.91).

Return to Piazza Santa Trinita and turn right along Via Porta Rossa. In the **Palazzo Davanzati** you can see how wealthy medieval and Renaissance Florentines once lived. Although this 14th-century palace presents a rather stern exterior, the rooms within are full of colour. Everything, including toilets and kitchens, has been preserved in period style; notice the lovely, lavish *trompe l'œil* frescoes in the Sala dei Pappagalli, and the various bedrooms and dining room complete with 15th-century furniture and paintings.

Florentine Men of Letters

DANTE ALIGHIERI (1265-1321), member of a Guelph family, was exiled by a faction of his party for the last 19 years of his life. His immortal poetic work, *The Divine Comedy*, describing a journey through Hell and Purgatory to arrive at last in Paradise, is one of the great landmarks of world literature. In it he juxtaposes divinely ordained political and social order with the ugly reality of the corrupt society around him.

Dante wrote his masterpiece not in the usual scholarly Latin, but in everyday language. His work established the Tuscan vernacular as Italy's language of literature.

PETRARCH (Francesco Petrarca, 1304-74), born in Arezzo, was the son of a Florentine lawyer. Poet, scholar, and a lifelong friend of Boccaccio, he was regarded as one of the most learned men of his time, and was instrumental in the rediscovery of classical literature that laid the basis for the flowering of Renaissance lyric poetry. He is best known for poems to 'Laura', in which he expresses an idealized and unrequited love.

GIOVANNI BOCCACCIO (1313-75) was a classical scholar and university lecturer, specializing in the works of Dante. Survivor of the Black Death, he used his experiences as the basis for his marvellous collection of prose tales, *The Decameron*. Written in an Italian still easily understood, the work is unrivalled for its gentle eroticism, humour and vivid characterization.

Some of Giotto's finest sculptures embellish the Bardi Chapel (right of the altar) in Santa Croce.

Beyond the palazzo on the left is the colonnaded Via Pellicceria, which leads to the **Piazza della Repubblica**. A couple of blocks of medieval buildings were cleared during the 19th century to create Florence's central square, which occupies the site of the original Roman forum of Florentia. Its stylish cafés fill up at lunchtime with office workers from the surrounding banks and businesses.

Turn right at the far side of the square, then left at the Mercato Nuovo along Via Porta Rossa, and continue on Via della Condotta to emerge into the Piazza San Firenze. This small square is dominated by the towering Baroque façade of San Firenze, which now houses the Law Courts. Take the Borgo dei Greci to the right of San Firenze, to its intersection with Via Bentaccordi. This is one of the few curved streets in medieval

Florence, and it owes its shape to the fact that it once ran around the outside of the Roman amphitheatre. Follow it around to the left until you emerge into the open space of Piazza Santa Croce.

PIAZZA SANTA CROCE

The vast expanse of Piazza Santa Croce formed one of the social and political hubs of Renaissance Florence. Lorenzo and Giuliano de' Medici used to stage lavish jousts here, and defiant Florentines turned out in force during the 1530 siege to watch or take part in their traditional football game. The buildings on the right-hand side of the square, with their cantilevered upper floors, were typical of the medieval city.

The Franciscan church of **Santa Croce** started off in 1228 as a modest chapel, situated – in true Franciscan tradition – in the middle of a working-class district. Arnolfo di Cambio, the architect of the Duomo, drew up the plans for a larger church, which was completed in the 14th century. The interior, beneath its open roof-beams, is grandly Gothic, while the style of the façade is 19th-century Neo-Gothic.

The church is the last resting place of some of the most illustrious figures in Italian history. Just inside the door on the right is the **tomb of Michelangelo**, designed by his first biographer, the 16th-century artist and architect Giorgio Vasari. Though he died in Rome, his body was brought back to Florence for the finest funeral in Florentine memory. The seated figures on the monument represent, from left to right, Painting, Sculpture and Architecture – the three realms of art in which he remains immortal.

The next tomb on the right wall, that of Dante Alighieri, lies empty, much to the dismay of the city. His body lies in Ravenna, where he died, and the Ravennese have never given in to Florentine pleas for its return. Further along are the tombs of Niccolo Machiavelli (1469-1527), civil servant, political theorist, historian and playwright (his famous book

The Prince – which gives advice on how to rule a state – has made his name, fairly or not, a synonym for hypocrisy and devilish cunning); and composer Gioacchino Rossini (1792-1868), whose masterpiece was the popular opera *The Barber of Seville*.

Opposite Michelangelo is the tomb of the Pisan genius Galileo Galilei (1564-1642), who is shown holding the telescope which he invented, while a plaque on the front of the tomb depicts the four moons of Jupiter he discovered by using it. On the same side of the church, beside the fourth column from the door, lies sculptor Lorenzo Ghiberti, creator of the famous Baptistery doors (see p.26). As you walk around this great church, you will be stepping over many fascinating 13th- and 14th-century tomb slabs set in the floor, their effigies badly worn but still visible.

In the nave, take a look at the splendid, late-15th-century marble pulpit sculptures, with scenes from the life of Saint Francis, and further up on the right, Donatello's sensitive *Annunciation* in grey *pietra serena*. A tranquil chapel in the left transept houses a coloured wooden Christ on the cross carved by Donatello. His friend Brunelleschi mockingly dismissed the sculpture as 'a peasant on the cross'.

The honeycomb of family chapels on either side of the high altar contains a wealth of frescoes dating from the 14th to 16th centuries. Immediately to the right of the altar, in the **Bardi Chapel**, you'll find Giotto's finest and arguably most moving works – scenes from the life of Saint Francis – painted around 1320.

The adjoining chapel, containing Giotto frescoes of the life of Saint John, belonged to the Peruzzi, rich bankers who donated most of the money for the church's imposing sacristy. Not long afterwards, the Peruzzi were ruined by the bankruptcy of Edward III of England (see p.15).

To the right of the church is the entrance to the **Museo dell'Opera di Santa Croce**. Cross the peaceful first cloister to reach the **Cappella dei Pazzi** (the highest of the three white plaques to the left of the façade shows the height of the 1966 flood waters). The infamous reputation of the Pazzi family is more than redeemed by this small chapel. One of the earliest and most exquisite Renaissance religious interiors, it was designed for the Pazzi family by Brunelleschi in 1430, and contains glazed terracotta decorations and tondos of the Four Evangelists and the 12 Apostles by Luca della Robbia.

The museum contains frescoes and statues that were removed from the church for preservation, but its greatest treasure is Cimabue's massive 13th-century painted crucifix, which was restored after near-destruction in the 1966 flood. Outside the museum, beneath the colonnade, is a memorial to Florence Nightingale, who was born in Florence in 1820 and named after the city. A doorway on the right leads into the tranquillity of the beautiful second cloister, where you can sit with only the sparrows for company and admire the graceful campanile above the top of the church.

There are two more interesting museums close to Santa Croce. The **Casa Buonarroti**, at Via Ghibellina 70, was bought by Michelangelo for his closest relatives. It contains letters, drawings, portraits of the great man, as well as a collection of 17th-century historical paintings illustrating his long and productive life. The exhibits include his famous sculptured relief, the *Madonna of the Staircase*, completed before the artist was 16. His astonishing *Battle of Lapiths and Centaurs* dates from around the same time.

The **Museo della Fondazione Horne**, situated near the river at Via de' Benci 6, is a superb little 15th-century palace, restored, lived in, and eventually bequeathed to Florence in 1916 by Englishman HP Horne. On display inside the museum is his priceless collection of paintings, drawings, sculptures, ceramics, furniture, coins and medals, and old household utensils.

The Oltrarno

The district on the far bank of the river is called the Oltrarno ('across the Arno'), and contains some of Florence's most attractive neighbourhoods. To get there, cross the river at the Ponte alla Carraia (the one downstream from Ponte Santa Trinita), turn right on Borgo San Frediano, then left into the Piazza del Carmine.

The square is overlooked by the unpretentious church of **Santa Maria del Carmine**, which houses some of the major frescoes in Florence. Masaccio and his teacher Masolino, commissioned by the wealthy merchant Felice Brancacci, worked from 1423 to 1427 on the decorations for the Brancacci Chapel at the end of the right transept. Masolino's own work is striking enough, but Masaccio's *The Tribute Money* and the *Expulsion of Adam and Eve from the Garden of Eden* raised the art of painting to a completely new level. His feeling for light and space, his dramatically stage-set figures, and the solidity of their forms, were considered little short of an inspired miracle. Nothing like them had been painted before – the Renaissance had arrived. Sadly, Masaccio died at the age of 27 before completing his work.

Florentine artists young and old made pilgrimages to the church to marvel at and learn from Masaccio's achievement. Michelangelo himself came here as a pupil to sketch the figures, and it was here, so the story goes, that a fellow student, Pietro Torrigiani, broke Michelangelo's nose, having been provoked by the latter's taunts at his clumsy drawings. Torrigiani, fearing Medici retribution for damaging their young protégé, fled abroad, eventually ending up in London where he sculpted the tomb of Henry VII in Westminster Abbey.

As you exit the church, turn right and follow Via Santa Monica and Via San Agostino to the attractive Piazza Santo Spirito. The market stalls and pavement cafés in this tree-lined square are as yet untouched by the tourist industry.

The modest façade rising above the back of the piazza is the church of **Santo Spirito**. A monastic foundation of the Augustinian order dating back to the 13th century, the present church was designed by Brunelleschi and built in the second half of the 15th century.

The bare, unfinished exterior conceals a masterpiece of Renaissance architectural harmony. The walls are lined with some 38 elegant side altars, while slender grey stone columns with Corinthian capitals, and an interplay of arches and vaulted aisles create an impression of tremendous space.

Next to the church, in the refectory of the original monastery, you can see the impressive 14th-century frescoes of *The Last Supper* and *The Crucifixion*, and the fine medieval and Renaissance sculptures of the Museo della Fondazione Romano. The Augustinian Order once ran a hospital, where the young Michelangelo – with the assent of the prior – perfected his knowledge of anatomy by dissecting the cadavers of dead patients.

Turn left on leaving Santo Spirito and follow the narrow Sdrucciolo dei Pitti to the Palazzo Pitti.

PALAZZO PITTI

This huge palace was built as a symbol of wealth and power by the Florentine merchant Luca Pitti, who wanted to impress his great rivals the Medici. It was begun in 1457, but was continuously enlarged until the 19th century. Pitti

The 'tondo' – a round painting or relief – became popular in Italy during the 15th century.

died in 1472, but the Medici were sufficiently impressed by his palace to buy it in 1549, after which it served as the official residence of the Medici and the later ruling families of Florence until 1919, when it was bequeathed to the country. The palace and grounds contain several museums and galleries, plus 4ha (10 acres) of ornate Italian gardens.

The sumptuous **Galleria Palatina** preserves the magnificent art collection of the Medici and Lorraine grand-dukes, just as the owners hung them – according to theme and personal preference rather than historical sequence. Priceless paintings hang four-high amid lavish gilt, stuccoed and frescoed decoration.

There are superb works by masters such as Titian, Rubens, Raphael, Botticelli, Velazquez and Murillo, exhibited in grandiose halls adorned with ceiling paintings of classical themes (the Hall of Mars, Hall of Venus, Hall of the Iliad).

Raphaels abound – make sure to see *La Gravida* (Pregnant Woman), his incisive portrait of *Cardinal Inghirami*, and the famous round painting, the *Madonna della Seggiola* (Madonna of the Chair). The model for the enigmatic *La Velata* (Veiled Woman) was Raphael's mistress.

The Hall of Mars is dominated by Rubens' powerful allegory, *The Consequences of War*, one of the most striking 17th-century Baroque paintings. See also his *Four Philosophers*, with a ruddy-faced likeness of Rubens himself standing on the left. The most memorable of several very fine Titians are *La Maddalena* (Mary Magdalen), the searching *Portrait of a Young Englishman* and *The Concert*.

The best of 19th- and 20th-century Italian art can be seen in the interesting **Galleria d'Arte Moderna** (Gallery of Modern Art), on the floor above the Palatina. Here you can discover the exciting works of Tuscany's own Impressionist movement, the *Macchiaioli* (or blotch-painters), of the 1860s. Fattori and Signorini are the most renowned Italian painters to look out for.

A Selection of Hotels and Restaurants in Florence

Recommended Hotels

During the high season of July and August, accommodation in Florence is at a premium, and you should try to book a room as far in advance as possible. In fact, reservations are strongly recommended any time between March and October, especially for the lower-priced hotels. However, if you do arrive in Florence without a reservation, the ITA office at Santa Maria Novella railway station will find a room for you (see ACCOMMODATION, pp.106-107).

As a basic guide, we have used the symbols below to indicate prices for a double room with bath, including breakfast:

▮▮▮▮▮	over L280,000
▮▮▮▮	L180,000-280,000
▮▮▮	L90,000-180,000
▮▮	L60,000-90,000
▮	below L60,000

FLORENCE

Annalena ▮▮▮

Via Romana, 34, 50125 Florence
Tel. (055) 222402, fax 219600
Stylish, spacious hotel on first floor of a former Medici palazzo, overlooking a splendid private garden. Located across from the Boboli Gardens. 20 rooms.

Astoria Pullman ▮▮▮▮

Via del Giglio, 50123 Florence
Tel. (055) 239 8095, fax 214632
Fine old Florentine palazzo, part of which dates from the 13th and 14th centuries, offering luxurious rooms. Centrally located close to the Duomo. 88 rooms.

Baglioni ▮▮▮▮

Piazza Unità Italiana
50123 Florence
Tel. (055) 23580, fax 235 8895
A spacious, well-run hotel just across the square from the railway station. This turn-of-the-century building boasts a roof-terrace restaurant offering fantastic views. 193 rooms.

Balestri ▮▮▮

Piazza Mentana, 7
50122 Florence
Tel. (055) 214743, fax 239 8042
Family-run hotel established in the 19th century, on river bank, close to the Uffizi. No frills, but homely and comfortable. 50 rooms.

Bandini
Piazza Santo Spirito, 9
50125 Florence
Tel. (055) 215308
An inexpensive treat on the south side of the Arno, oozing with old-fashioned charm. 10 rooms.

Beacci Tornabuoni
Via dei Tornabuoni, 3
50123 Florence
Tel. (055) 212645, fax 283594
Classic Florentine hotel in a 14th-century palazzo in the town centre. Old-fashioned elegance with a homely atmosphere. 29 rooms.

Bellettini
Via dei Conti, 7, 50123 Florence
Tel. (055) 213561, fax 283551
Pleasant hotel with cheerfully decorated rooms, near the San Lorenzo street market. 27 rooms.

Bernini Palace
Piazza San Firenze
50122 Florence
Tel. (055) 288621, fax 268272
Atmospheric hotel at the back of the Palazzo Vecchio. 86 rooms.

Boston
Via Guelfa, 68, 50129 Florence
Tel. (055) 496747, fax 470934
Family-run hotel a few blocks from the railway station. Rooms small but comfortable. 16 rooms.

Le Due Fontane
Piazza della SS Annunziata, 14
50122 Florence
Tel. (055) 280086, fax 294461
Comfortable, recently renovated rooms overlooking the most beautiful square in Florence. 51 rooms.

Excelsior
Piazza Ognissanti, 3
50123 Florence
Tel. (055) 264201, fax 210278
Old-fashioned elegance in Florence's flagship hotel, on the banks of the Arno. Plush carpets, chaise-longues and spacious bathrooms in the rooms. 192 rooms.

Grand
Piazza Ognissanti, 1
50123 Florence
Tel. (055) 288781, fax 217400
Sister hotel to the Excelsior – both are run by the CIGA group. Similar level of luxury, with Renaissance-style frescoes. 107 rooms.

Jennings-Riccioli
Corso Tintori, 7, 50122 Florence
Tel. (055) 244751
Famous hotel on the banks of the river, which has absorbed the old Pension Simi, the original of the Pension Bertolini in EM Forster's classic novel, *A Room With a View*. Room 21 is reputedly *the* 'room with a view'. 55 rooms.

Kraft ■■■■
Via Solferino, 2, 50123 Florence
Tel. (055) 284273, fax 239 8267
Friendly hotel on the banks of the Arno. Many rooms overlook the river. Swimming pool. 68 rooms.

Liana ■■
Via V Alfieri, 18, 50121 Florence
Tel. (055) 245303, fax 234 4596
Formerly the British Embassy. Rooms overlooking a shady garden in a quiet area. 18 rooms.

Loggiato dei Serviti ■■■
Piazza della SS Annunziata, 3
50122 Florence
Tel. (055) 289592; fax 289595
A 16th-century loggia houses this hotel, beneath the vaulted ceilings of a former Servite monastery on a beautiful piazza. 29 rooms.

Monna Lisa ■■■■
Borgo Pinti, 27, 50121 Florence
Tel. (055) 247 9751, fax 247 9755
Renaissance palace, with original wooden ceilings and red-brick floors. Small rooms overlooking a central garden. 20 rooms.

Nuova Italia ■■
Via Faenza, 26, 50123 Florence
Tel. (055) 268430, fax 210941
One of many basic but comfortable hotels in the area east of the railway station. 20 rooms.

Plaza e Lucchesi ■■■■
Lungarno della Zecca Vecchia, 38
50122 Florence
Tel. (055) 26236, fax 248 0921
Elegant and friendly hotel overlooking the river, a few blocks upstream from the Uffizi. 97 rooms.

Quisisana e Pontevecchio ■■■
Lungarno Archibusieri, 4
50122 Florence
Tel. (055) 216692, fax 268303
A fine old 19th-century *pensione*, rich in character, and enjoying a central location beside the river. It was used as the setting for the film of EM Forster's *A Room With A View.* 37 rooms.

Regency ■■■■■
Piazza M. D'Azeglio
50121 Florence
Tel. (055) 245247, fax 245247
19th-century style town house furnished with antiques and situated in a leafy, quiet backwater to the east of the centre. 33 rooms.

Rigatti ■■
Lungarno Gen. Diaz, 2
50122 Florence
Tel. (055) 213022
A fine old Italian *pensione* with large, old-fashioned rooms and a very pleasant terrace overlooking the Arno. 28 rooms.

Recommended Restaurants

Central Florence is well supplied with cafés, bars, pizzerias, and restaurants, but they are often expensive. The further away from the tourist attractions you go, the lower the price. In a café, it is more expensive to sit at a table, especially an outside table, than to stand at the bar, as you will be paying for waiter service. Most restaurant bills will include a service charge (*servizio*), and in this case it is usual simply to leave the small change for the waiter. If service is not included, leave a tip of around 10 percent.

Below is a list of restaurants recommended by Berlitz; if you find other places worth including, we'd be pleased to hear from you. Reservations are recommended for the more expensive establishments. As a basic guide, we have used the following symbols to give an indication of the price of a three-course meal for two, excluding wine:

▮▮▮▮	over L120,000
▮▮▮	L80,000-120,000
▮▮	L40,000-80,000
▮	below L40,000

FLORENCE

Alle Mossacce ▮–▮▮

Via del Proconsolo, 55r
Tel. (055) 294361
Traditional *trattoria* with paper tablecloths and brusque, bustling waiters. The food is pure Tuscany – try a meal of *crostini* (toast spread with liver and anchovy paste), *ribollita* (vegetable soup thickened with bread) and *spezzatino alla fiorentina* (beef and tomato stew), washed down with red wine. Closed Saturday and Sunday, August.

Caffè Concerto ▮▮▮

Lungarno Cristoforo Colombo, 7
Tel. (055) 677377
Italian-style *nouvelle cuisine* in a refined riverside restaurant. The fine food is complemented by a wood-floored dining room fitted with antique wooden tables and chairs. Closed Sunday.

Caffè Gilli ■■

Piazza della Repubblica, 39r
Tel. (055) 239 6310
Founded over 250 years ago, the Caffè Gilli is arguably the plushest of all the piazza's cafés, somehow redolent of a bygone era, with its silver service and impeccable waiters. The establishment is famous for its cocktails, but it also boasts delicious sweets and pastries. Closed on Tuesdays.

Caffè Paszkowski ■■

Piazza della Repubblica, 6r.
No phone number
Another luxurious café and terrace, with a grand piano right on the pavement, the Caffè Paszkowski is a popular lunch spot for local office workers, serving salads, pasta, sandwiches and sweets. Closed Monday.

Cantinone del Gallo Nero ■–■■

Via Santo Spirito, 6r
Tel. (055) 218898
An inexpensive lunch spot with friendly communal tables, the Cantinone del Gallo Nero offers a large selection of *antipasti*, of various *crostini,* and good hearty traditional dishes, such as *ribollita* and *salsicce e fagioli* (a dish of sausage and beans). The restaurant is closed on Mondays.

Il Cestello ■■■■

Hotel Excelsior
Piazza Ognissanti, 3
Tel. (055) 264201
Fine old Florentine dining room, with roof garden tables in summer. The mix of local and Mediterranean dishes varies with the seasons. Closed in May.

Il Cibreo ■■■–■■■■

Via dei Macci, 118r
Tel. (055) 234 1100
Simple, *trattoria*-style restaurant that adopts a modern approach to beautifully presented classic Florentine dishes – *pappa al pomodoro* (a thick soup of bread and tomato, flavoured with garlic and basil), *piccione farcito con mostarda di frutta* (pigeon stuffed with mixed fruit), *palombo giovane alla livornese* (Livorno-style pigeon). Magnificent desserts. The *ristorante* section is more expensive and more formal. Closed Sunday and Monday.

Coco Lezzone ■■–■■■

Via del Parioncino, 26r
Tel. (055) 287178
Popular *trattoria* serving classic Florentine food on tables covered with red and white checked cloths. Try the tasty pasta with *porcini* (wild mushrooms). Closed Tuesday, Sunday dinner and in August.

Dino ■■–■■■
Via Ghibellina, 51r
Tel. (055) 241452
A fine, traditional menu, inspired in part by the peasant dishes of Tuscany, in part by the noble banquets of the Medici – from *trippa alla fiorentina* (tripe in tomato sauce with parmesan) to *anguille del Papa Martino IV* (eels à la Pope Martin IV!). Closed Sunday evening, Monday, and in August.

Enoteca Pinchiori ■■■■
Via Ghibellina, 87
Tel. (055) 242777
One of the best and most famous restaurants in Italy, with one of the world's greatest wine cellars. The gourmet menu blends French and Tuscan influences – *sella di coniglio al forno* (roast saddle of rabbit), *filetti de triglia cotti sulla pelle* (fillet of red mullet), *costolette di agnello con timballo di legumi e composta di pomodri verdi* (lamb cutlets with vegetable timbale and green tomatoes). Dress formal. Closed Sunday and lunchtime Monday.

Il Fiorino ■■■–■■■■
Grand Hotel
Piazza Ognissanti, 1
Tel. (055) 288781
Interesting Mediterreanean *nouvelle cuisine* served in a stylish and sophisticated setting. The fixed menu 'Quick Lunch' is good value. Closed in May.

Giubbe Rosse ■■
Piazza della Repubblica, 13-14r
Tel. (055) 212280
This historic café was once a famous meeting place for the city's intellectual *élite*. It is still trendy and popular with tourists, and offers a full American breakfast. Closed Wednesday.

Harry's Bar ■■–■■■
Lungarno A. Vespucci, 22
Tel. (055) 239 6700
A sophisticated night-spot which follows the time-honoured custom of cocktail hour. The menu includes international fare such as steak, scampi, club sandwiches, salads, and also a couple of local dishes. Closed Sunday.

I Che C'è C'è ■■
Via Magalotti, 11r
Tel. (055) 216589
A rough translation of the name might be 'we've got what we've got' – in other words, ask what today's special is. It's a popular and friendly establishment that serves good Florentine fare such as *ribollita*, *stracotto* and *coniglio ripieno* (rabbit stuffed with spinach and egg). Closed Monday.

La Loggia ▮▮▮
Piazzale Michelangelo
Tel. (055) 234 2832
The food is fine, but the view over the city is the big attraction. It can be overwhelmed by coach parties (especially in high season); nevertheless, it is worth waiting for a table. Closed Wednesday.

Osteria N.1 ▮▮▮
Via del Moro, 18-22r
Tel. (055) 284897/294318
Delicious dishes based on various traditional Tuscan recipes such as *salame toscano con fichi* (Tuscan salami with figs), *sfogliatine di ricotta al basilico* (pasta pockets filled with ricotta cheese and basil) or *la noce de vitella tartufata* (veal with black truffle sauce). The restaurant is closed on Sundays.

Pennello ▮▮
Via Dante Alighieri, 4r
Tel. (055) 294848
Old-style *trattoria* with a magnificent spread of *antipasti* for lunch, conveniently close to all the main attractions. Closed Sunday evening, Monday, and in August.

Sabatini ▮▮▮▮
Via dei Panzani, 9/A
Tel. (055) 211559/282802
This well-known Florentine institution has been equally frequented by locals and visitors since 1930. Renowned for its numerous classic dishes such as *antipasti alla Sabatini* (marinated fish and vegetables), *risotto con punti di asparagi* (rice with asparagus tips), and *scallopini di vitello con carciofi* (escalope of veal with artichokes). Closed Monday.

Sostanza ▮▮–▮▮▮
Via della Porcellana, 25r
Tel. (055) 212691
This old-fashioned 'diner' was established in Florence in 1869. It serves a traditional and hearty country fare such as minestrone, tripe, fried chicken, *stracotto* (beef stew with tomatoes and red wine) or *bistecca fiorentina*. The restaurant is closed on Saturdays, Sundays and in August.

La Vittoria ▮▮▮
Via della Fonderia,52r
Tel. (055) 225 657
This is a highly respected seafood restaurant. Simply furnished, it serves whatever is available fresh from the market that day – *seppia* (cuttlefish), *coda di rospo* (monkfish tail), *rombo* (turbot), scampi, lobster, crab and a large variety of shellfish – although the less adventurous diners may well prefer the more usual fried or grilled whitefish. Closed Wednesday.

Sixteen sumptuous rooms house the **Museo degli Argenti** (Silverware Museum), where you can admire some of the Medici's most cherished jewellery, gold, silver, cameos, crystal, ivory, furniture and porcelain, including Lorenzo Il Magnifico's priceless collection of 16 exquisite antique vases. The room in which they are displayed is the biggest surprise of all, for its 17th-century frescoes create a dizzying optical illusion of extra height and depth. A red-cloaked Lorenzo appears in three of the allegorical murals.

Once you have had your fill of the galleries, take a relaxing stroll in the delightful **Giardino di Boboli**, an Italian pleasure-garden of arbours and cypress-lined avenues dotted here and there with graceful statuary, lodges, grottoes and fountains. Laid out over the hillside where the palace's huge stones were quarried, the park was originally built for Cosimo I's nature-loving consort, Eleonora of Toledo.

The entrance to the gardens is at the back of the palace

The rusticated walls of the Palazzo Pitti house some of the finest galleries in Florence.

courtyard, and leads to the amphitheatre, which has a fine view of the palace and the city beyond. Up the hill behind it you will find the Vasca del Nettuno (Neptune Fountain) and the Casino del Cavaliere, housing the Museo delle Porcellane, a fine porcelain collection. Away to the right, at the end of a long cypress avenue, is the unique Piazzale dell'Isolotto, an idyllic island of greenery, fountains and sculpture set in an ornamental pond; to the left is the coffee shop, which enjoys a pleasant view of Florence. Returning downhill, head right below the amphitheatre to see the Grotta Grande, a man-made cave, as well as the famous statue of Cosimo I's court jester, a pot-bellied dwarf, riding on the back of a turtle.

The Boboli Garden offers the chance of a pleasant stroll after exploring the Palazzo Pitti.

SAN MINIATO

The church of San Miniato is arguably the most beautiful in Florence, and enjoys a magnificent hilltop location. The easy way to get there is to take a number 13 bus to Piazzale Michelangelo, but a more interesting alternative is to walk along the city walls.

From the Palazzo Pitti, return to the river and turn right along the Via dei Bardi. Where the buildings on the left stop, allowing a view of the river, you will see an archway in the corner on the right. Go through the arch and follow the Costa dei Magnoli up a

steep hill to the **Forte di Belvedere**. This 16th-century fortification offers a panoramic view over the city; its terraces are used for exhibitions of modern sculpture.

Take the road that runs along the foot of the old city wall, which drops down to the gateway of Porta San Miniato. Here, turn right and follow the narrow road and the steps above it to the main road, and go along to the right until you find the stairs leading up to **San Miniato al Monte**.

Saint Minias, an early Christian martyred in the 3rd century AD, is said to have carried his own severed head up to this hilltop and set it down on the spot where the church was later built. During the siege of 1530, when the Emperor Charles V's Spanish gunners pounded away at the city, San Miniato was well within range and might have been blown to pieces. However, Michelangelo, who was in charge of the Florentine defences, had a temporary fortress hastily built around the site, and protected the bell-tower with mattresses and bales of wool. Easily overlooked if you're short of time, San Miniato is nonetheless one of the city's most romantic churches.

Rebuilt in the early 11th century, it is a remarkable example of Florentine-style Romanesque architecture. The superb green and white marble façade contains a 13th-century mosaic representing Christ flanked by Saint Minias and the Virgin Mary.

The interior has all the splendour of a Byzantine basilica, with its wealth of richly inlaid marble and mosaic decorations. Note the painted wooden ceiling, and the nave's 13th-century marble floor. See also the fine 15th-century Chapel of the Cardinal of Portugal (who died in Florence), and some 14th-century frescoes in the sacristy.

Relax awhile on the terrace and enjoy the view, or adjourn to the little shop and bar run by the resident Benedictine order, where a white-robed monk will sell you anything from honey and herb liqueurs to a postcard or a cold drink.

Day Trips from Florence

Many travel agencies offer a wide range of coach tours, both conducted and unaccompanied. The tourist office (see p.127) also organizes local tours. Regional bus services (see p.128) cover the whole of Tuscany, while the orange city buses are useful for shorter excursions. Here are a few ideas for places that can be reached from Florence in an hour or less by car or public transport.

FIESOLE

A winding road climbs for some 8km (5 miles) through the fields and villas north of Florence to the charming little hilltop town of Fiesole (to get there, take a number 7 bus from Santa Maria Novella station). An ancient Etruscan stronghold and later a Roman settlement, it provides a welcome escape from the summer heat of the city, and offers wonderful views over Florence and the Arno Valley.

The bus drops you in the town square, Piazza Mino da Fiesole, which has a tourist information office and a couple of pleasant open-air cafés. Opposite the bus stop is Fiesole's cathedral. Founded in 1028 and completed during the 13th and 14th centuries, **San Romolo** was totally restored in the 19th century, leaving it with a rather drab exterior. Its aggressively Tuscan campanile, which is visible for miles around, dates back to 1213. A Byzantine atmosphere pervades the interior, which contains the Capella Salutati, with two works by Mino da Fiesole – a tabernacle showing the Virgin with Saints, and the tomb of Bishop Salutati.

To the right of the cathedral is the arched entrance to the **Roman Theatre** and archaeological site. Apart from a few fragments of a defensive wall, hardly a trace of Fiesole's Etruscan occupation remains. The Roman ruins are rather more impressive, however, with the well-preserved theatre dating from around 100 BC and seating some 2,500 spectators.

Half is original and half has been restored, and it is still used today for performances of plays and music during the *Estate Fiesolana* (Summer Festival; see p.91). Below the theatre are the remains of Roman baths, and a temple. A small but interesting Archaeological Museum is housed in a replica of the temple just inside the entrance.

Cypresses and country villas are dotted across the hillsides around the town of Fiesole.

Back on the square, turn right and follow a steep but picturesque lane uphill to the church of **San Francesco** and its tiny monastery. The views of Florence from the terrace below the church are memorable, and the monastery, with its peaceful little cloisters, is enchanting. A wooded park offers a choice of footpaths back down the hill.

Rather than take the bus back to Florence, you might enjoy a pleasant walk downhill to the Mugnone valley and into town – allow two hours to return to the city centre. From the bottom end of the square, head down the main road but immediately fork right down the very steep **Via Vecchia Fiesolana**, which was the original road to the town. It zig-zags down the hillside between country villas and old stone walls, with breathtaking views of Florence below, the Duomo prominent above a sea of red-tiled roofs.

You rejoin the main road at the 15th-century Dominican church and monastery of **San Domenico**. This is where Fra Angelico took his vows; his fine fresco of *The Crucifixion* adorns the Chapter House. Just before the church, a right turn at the traffic lights leads in five minutes to the **Badia Fiesolana**, which served as Fiesole's cathedral until 1028. It was rebuilt at the behest of Cosimo Il Vecchio in the 15th century, and is a little gem of Renaissance architecture.

Immediately beyond San Domenico, fork right on Via Giovanni Boccaccio, shaded by cypress trees, which winds down gently to the small River Mugnone, and on into the suburbs of Florence. Where the riverbank path ends, cross the bridge and turn right, and you will soon find yourself in the Piazza delle Cure, from which a number 1 or 7 bus (or another half-hour's walk) will return you to the city centre.

MEDICI VILLAS

Scattered around the edges of Florence are the former country estates of the Medici family, where they farmed the land, built luxurious villas, and laid out ornamental gardens. A number of these villas and their grounds have been restored and opened to the public, and can easily be reached by public transport.

Nearest to town, about 5km (3 miles) from the city centre, is the **Villa Medicea di Careggi** (bus number 14C from Santa Maria Novella). This was Cosimo Il Vecchio's favourite house; he often retreated to this peaceful spot to rest and study, and eventually, to die. His son Piero and grandson Lorenzo Il Magnifico both died here too. The villa itself can only be visited by special permission (it is used by the local hospital), but you can explore the pleasant wooded parklands round about it. (Ask at the tourist office for details.)

A few kilometres further out, on the road to Sesto Fiorentino, lies the **Villa Medicea La Petraia** (bus number 28; gardens open 9am to dusk; villa closes one hour before gardens; closed Mondays). The hilltop house was originally a castle, but was converted during the late 16th century for grand-duke Ferdinando I. A glass roof was built over the courtyard in the 19th century so that it could be used as a ballroom, the walls of which are adorned with 17th-century frescoes glorifying the Medici. The attractive gardens contain a fountain with a copy of Giambologna's famous bronze figure of Venus wringing water from her hair, symbolizing the city of Florence and the waters of the Arno (the original is preserved in the villa).

A short walk down the hill from La Petraia will bring you to the **Villa Medicea di Castello** (gardens open from 9am to dusk), which was bought around 1477 by Lorenzo Il Magnifico's cousins, Giuliano and Lorenzo di Pierfrancesco – the two minor members of the Medici family who were immortalized in marble by Michelangelo in the New Sacristy of San Lorenzo (see p.44). The villa is not open to the public, but that doesn't matter – it is the splendid gardens which are the main attraction. These gardens were commissioned by Cosimo I in 1541 to celebrate the prosperity of Tuscany under the rule of the Medici, with tableaux symbolizing the landscape and seasons. The highlights are the superb fountain, with a bronze of *Hercules and Anteus* by Ammannati; the Grotto degli Animali, an artificial cave inhabited by sculpted birds and animals (the original bronze birds by Giambologna can be seen in the Bargello in Florence; see p.30); and at the top of the gardens, the colossal figure of *Enero* (January) rising shivering from a pool, symbolizing the Appenine mountains in winter.

The grandest and most impressive of the Medici country houses is the **Villa di Poggio a Caiano** (COPIT bus from Santa Maria Novella station; villa open 9am-5pm/1.30pm on Sunday; gardens 9am to one hour before dusk; closed Mondays). This villa was the favourite residence of Lorenzo Il Magnifico, and it was built especially for him in the 1480s. The richly decorated rooms culminate in the imposing *salone*, a great hall adorned with splendid 16th-century allegorical frescoes that commemorate both Lorenzo Il Magnifico and Cosimo Il Vecchio.

PISA

Roughly 80km (50 miles) downstream from Florence lies Pisa, the birthplace of Galileo, and home of the famous Leaning Tower. The city was a flourishing commercial centre during the Middle Ages, until the silting up of the Arno estuary left it stranded. The most conspicuous legacy of Pisa's wealthy and powerful past, and what everybody comes to to admire, are the architectural wonders of the buildings of the **Campo dei Miracoli** (Field of Miracles) – the Duomo, the Battistero, and, of course, the Leaning Tower.

The centrepiece of the Field of Miracles is the **Duomo**, the most important and influential Romanesque building in Tuscany, and the first to use the much-copied facing of grey and white marble bands. It was begun around 1063 and completed by 1118 (its fine bronze doors also date from the 12th century). The striped decoration is repeated in the vast interior, which also boasts an ornate wooden ceiling. The cathedral's masterpiece, however, is undoubtedly the magnificent carved pulpit by Giovanni Pisano (1302-10).

The **Battistero** (Baptistery) was started in 1152 but not completed until the 14th century. Its unusual turban-dome caps a circular gallery of Gothic windows, as well as a lower storey of Romanesque arches. The sparsely decorated interior contains a superb pulpit and baptismal font.

However, it is the world-famous, 57m (187ft) **Campanile** of the cathedral which really captures the eye, just as beautiful and delicate as carved ivory, and now leaning out of plumb by 4.5m (15ft). It was begun in 1173, and began to lean when only three of the eight storeys had been completed, as the ground beneath the Campo is a waterlogged sand – hardly ideal foundation material (the Duomo and Baptistery are also slightly out of true). Various architects attempted to correct the lean as construction work continued, resulting in a slight bend by the time of the tower's completion around 1350. It has been closed indefinitely since 1990 for preservation work. The latest plan (1993) entails fixing 670 tons of lead ingots to the foundations on the side

The leaning Tower of Pisa was originally built as a bell-tower for the neighbouring cathedral.

opposite the lean, to act as a counterweight. Only time will tell whether gravity or ingenuity will win out.

Behind these mighty monuments stretches the walled-in **Camposanto**, a unique 13th-century, cloister-like cemetery, the walls of which are covered with remarkable 14th-15th-century frescoes, some by Benozzo Gozzoli. These were badly damaged during World War II bombing raids, and restoration work has not been completed yet.

It's hard to believe today, but Pisa was once on the River Arno's estuary (which now lies 10km/6½ miles away at Marina di Pisa). A flourishing sea-port colonized by the Greeks, then settled by the Etruscans, and later by the Romans, it had become a rich and powerful naval republic by the 12th century, and home to one of Italy's first universities. Long desired and fought over as an outlet to the sea by an envious Florence, the city was forcibly taken in 1406. Yet only 15 years later its harbour lay silted-up and redundant.

SIENA

Siena, about 48km (30 miles) south of Florence, is still essentally a medieval city. Its walls enclose a maze of narrow, winding streets that have survived virtually unchanged since the 16th century. It can be reached easily from Florence by SITA's express bus service (see pp.128-129).

As you approach Siena along a road cut through a succession of undulating hills covered with a rich, reddish-brown soil, you'll understand how the artists' pigment, 'burnt sienna', came by its name. The city itself, in contrast to Florence's dull browns and greys, is a wonderful marriage of brick and stone, all rich reds and warm pinks.

Imposing Gothic architecture prevails within the city walls, from the 14th-century Palazzo Pubblico with its graceful and slender Torre del Mangia, to the grand cathedral and many fine palazzi.

The heart of the city is the huge, sloping, and fan-shaped **Piazza del Campo**, where the exciting Palio horse-race (see p.84) takes place each summer. Its atmosphere of aristocratic grandeur befits the proud Ghibelline stronghold that Siena once was. Founded by the descendants of Remus (whose twin brother Romulus founded Rome), this proudest and most stubbornly independent of Tuscan cities did not fall under Florentine sway until the year 1555.

In the **Palazzo Pubblico**, you can see Simone Martini's giant frescoes of the *Maestà* (Christ in Majesty, 1315), and the *Condottiere Guidoriccio da Fogliano* (1328) on his richly caparisoned horse; note also Ambrogio Lorenzetti's impressive allegorical frescoes, *Good and Bad Government* (1339), one of the largest medieval paintings with a non-religious theme.

Siena's Piazza del Campo is the atmospheric setting for the exciting Palio horse-races.

A peaceful corner for a picture-seller among the medieval back streets of San Gimignano.

Wander through the picturesque, winding streets to the great Gothic **Duomo**, with its striking black-and-white striped exterior – a motif repeated in the city's coat of arms. The attractions within include the inlaid marble floor, a splendid sculptured pulpit, and Pinturicchio's colourful historical frescoes in the adjoining Piccolomini Library, while Duccio's splendid *Maestà* (1308) can be admired in the neighbouring Museo dell' Opera del Duomo.

Siena produced some of the leading Italian painters of the 13th and 14th centuries, and many of their works are on display in the city's art gallery, the **Pinacoteca** (housed in the Palazzo Buonsignori).

If you're in Italy at the right time of year (summer), it's worth going out of your way to see the **Palio**, a traditional bareback horse-race that has been held in the Piazza del Campo since the 13th century. Try to reserve a seat in the stand or a place on a balcony, as the crush and excitement down on the Campo can be uncomfortable. After a stately procession of colourful pages, men-at-arms, and knights and flag-twirlers dressed in 15th-century costumes, ten fiercely competitive bareback riders, each representing a different *contrada* (city ward), battle it out over three laps of the piazza. The winner is awarded the coveted *Palio* – a painted silken standard. The only rule is that the riders must not interfere with each other's reins; otherwise, anything goes. As you watch this violent spectacle, you may well feel that you've been transported back to Renaissance times.

SAN GIMIGNANO

The walled medieval town of San Gimignano is one of the most evocative and picturesque in Italy. Strategically perched on a hilltop, its skyline bristles with the angular outlines of traditional Tuscan tower-houses. At one time the town could boast over 70 of them – it was a matter of prestige to build the tallest tower possible. Today, just over a dozen remain, but that's still more than enough to make it the best-preserved medieval town in Tuscany, and to earn it the proud descriptive appellation '*delle belle torri*' (of the beautiful towers).

Here you can stroll through streets and squares barely changed since Dante arrived as a Florentine envoy in 1300. The 12th-century **Collegiata** church is filled with impressive frescoes, including a 14th-century *Last Judgement*, and *The Martyrdom of Saint Sebastian* by Gozzoli. Don't miss the Capella di Santa Fina, decorated with elegant Ghirlandaio murals depicting San Gimignano's towers in the background. Saint Fina, only 15 years old when she died, was a 13th-century mystic who was adopted as one of the town's patron saints.

Visit the 13th-14th-century **Palazzo del Popolo**, with its 54m (177ft) tower, a superb little courtyard, and unusual frescoes of hunting and courtly love, before walking up to the **Rocca** (citadel) for a panoramic view over the town and valley. In the 13th-century church of **Sant'Agostino**, take a look at the fresco in the choir by Gozzoli depicting *Scenes from the Life of Saint Augustine*, filled with details of everyday life in medieval Italy.

What to Do

Shopping

Italians in general and Florentines in particular have always held craftsmanship in high regard, and the city's shops are famed for the quality of their merchandise, especially jewellery, leather goods, antiques, straw goods, and fashion.

Shop windows compete for your attention along smart, expensive Via dei Tornabuoni and Via de' Calzaiuoli, and in the neighbouring side-streets, and window-shopping is alaways a pleasure. English is understood in the majority of shops in the city centre. **Markets** (see p.89) are held daily in the Mercato Nuovo, Piazza San Lorenzo and Piazza Ghiberti, and on Tuesday mornings in the Cascine park.

Shops are open 8.30/9am-1pm and 4-8pm. From 15 June to 15 September, all shops close on Saturday afternoons (on Monday morning the rest of the year). Food shops are closed on Wednesdays as well.

Best Buys

Antiques and reproductions: antique shops cluster around the Borgo Ognissanti, Via della Vigna Nuova and Via della Spada, and in Via Maggio and Borgo San Jacopo in the Oltrarno. Specializing largely in furniture, paintings and decorations, none of them are cheap. A major international antique fair is held biennially at the Palazzo Strozzi (September-October).

Bric-a-brac addicts will find a permanent, modest-sized flea market on Piazza dei Ciompi, though the prices are a bit on the high side (the market is open daily in full season).

If you can't afford an old master, treat yourself to a good reproduction, a Florentine speciality. You can get a full-size version of any of your favourite statue or any piece of 'antique' furniture made to order. Framed, 18th-century prints of Florence are good buys, especially in the shops around Piazza del Duomo. You can also look for unframed prints in the San Lorenzo market.

The busy Via dei Calzaiuoli is one of Florence's principal shopping streets.

Ceramics and glassware: expensive, high quality table china, bright ceramic ornaments and statuettes cater for every taste; they are mostly produced at nearby Sesto Fiorentino. Attractive functional glassware, often very cheap, comes from Empoli or Pisa.

Fashion: Florentine designers are on a par with those from Paris, Rome and London, and couturier's shows are held in the city twice a year. Exclusive designs are pricey, but still far cheaper than they would be at home. There's always a marvellous selection of designer accessories such as gloves, scarves and belts.

Gold and silver: designer gold jewellery is terribly expensive, but simpler items like gold or silver charms are reasonably priced. The place to window-shop is, of course, over the Arno, along the Ponte Vecchio, with its centuries-old jewellers' shops, each window more tempting than the last.

The work of Florentine silversmiths, sometimes inspired by ancient motifs, is invariably

Florence is famed for its traditional crafts, such as leatherwork and ceramics.

beautiful and practical. Look for pill-boxes, napkin rings, photo frames, cruet sets, sugar bowls and candlesticks.

Inlays and mosaics: a Florentine speciality, the art of wood inlay or *intarsio* was perfected during the Renaissance. By the end of the 16th century, semi-precious stones were often used in the inlays. The craft still flourishes, and you'll see impressive modern examples for sale in Lungarno Torrigiani, Via Guicciardini and Piazza Santa Croce. Larger items like tables are inevitably expensive; small, framed 'naïve' pictures of birds, flowers, Tuscan landscapes or views of Florence are charming curiosities, and comparatively cheap.

Leather: Florence is well-known for its quality leather goods – this is the home town of Gucci. Its tell-tale smell around San Lorenzo and Santa Croce will lead you to shops and stalls selling everything from handbags and luggage to wallets and gloves. Shoe shops are concentrated along Via de' Calzaiuoli.

Don't miss the Leather Guild in Piazza Santa Croce, housed in part of the former Franciscan monastery. Here you'll see apprentices cutting, tooling and stamping traditional motifs. A tempting selection of their work is on sale.

The best buys are gloves, belts, purses, wallets and boxes of all shapes and sizes. Handbags are tempting but almost always expensive, and the difference between shop and market prices is small. As a free bonus, you can usually have your initials stamped in gold on any purchase.

Stationery: Florence has been a major centre of printing and bookbinding for centuries, and this is reflected in shops selling specialized writing goods such as designer pens and desk-sets, hand-made marbled papers and envelopes, personalized notebooks and filofaxes.

Straw goods: the stalls of the Mercato Nuovo, also known as the Straw Market, sell bags, hats, mats and souvenirs made out of woven straw, another Florentine speciality.

Street Markets

The biggest and most popular market is **San Lorenzo**, which caters to both tourists and locals, and sells everything from tools to crocodile handbags. Here you'll find clothing, shoes and leatherware, often at bargain prices. Several stalls even accept credit cards, and many take traveller's cheques and will mail purchases to anywhere in the world. The huge archways stretching over Via dell'Ariento belong to the **Mercato Centrale**, the central food market, bulging to the seams with fresh fruit and vegetables, meat, fish and game.

The **Mercato Nuovo**, or **Straw Market** is conveniently located, halfway between Piazza della Repubblica and the Ponte Vecchio. Housed beneath a loggia built in 1547, a score of stalls offer attractive straw-work bags and sun-hats, semi-precious stone trinkets, glass-mosaic jewellery, miniature reproductions of the *David* of Michelangelo, gilt-patterned wooden articles, and other souvenirs.

A daily **flea market** operates in Piazza dei Ciompi, selling the usual mix of junk and bric-a-brac. A genuine antiques market is also held in the same spot, and takes place on the last Sunday of each month.

A huge weekly market sets up every Tuesday morning in **Cascine** park, selling all kinds of goods. It's especially good for cheap clothes and shoes.

Entertainment

Whatever the time of year, there's always something interesting going on in Florence. Information on current events can be found on the weekly 'what's on' posters throughout the city, and in the useful monthly publication, *Calendar of Events in Florence and its Province,* available from the tourist office. There are also weekly entertainment listings in the weekend editions of *La Nazione* and *La Repubblica* papers. For up-to-the-minute information on all events, and to get some tickets, contact *Box Office*, Via della Pergola 10r, tel. (055) 242361; or approach directly the Teatro Comunale, Corso Italia 16, tel. (055) 2779236; or the Teatro Verdi, Via Ghibellina 101, tel. (055) 212320.

Music and Theatre

Concerts are a year-round feature of Florentine cultural life. Evening concerts are held in the **Boboli Gardens** (see p.73) in July and August; organ recitals in historic churches in September and October. During June, July and August, nearby **Fiesole** (see pp.76-78) offers the *Estate Fiesolana* festival of concerts, ballet, drama and film, with many of the events staged at the restored Roman theatre. In June and September, the beautiful Medici villa at **Poggio a Caiano** (see p.80) serves as the setting for plays, as well as concerts.

Calendar of Events

25 March – Annunciation Day: city celebrations, fair in Piazza della Santissima Annunziata.

March/April – Easter Sunday *Scoppio del Carro* (Explosion of the Cart): cart full of fireworks in Piazza del Duomo is set off by burning 'dove' released from the high altar at midday mass.

23 May – Ascension Day *Festa del Grillo* (Festival of the Cricket): fair in Cascine Park. Crickets in tiny cages sold to be set free.

Mid-May to **mid-June** – *Maggio Musical* (Musical May): programme of opera, ballet and concerts throughout the city.

June to **September** – *Estate Fiesolana:* summer festival of music, ballet and theatre in Fiesole.

24 and **28 June** – Feast of St John the Baptist, Patron Saint of Florence: fireworks and two football games. *Giuoco del Calci*: traditional rowdy football game in 16th-century costume, in Piazza della Signoria and Piazza Santa Croce. Fireworks in Piazzale Michelangelo on 24th.

2 July and **16 August** – *Palio di Siena*: historic pageant and horse-race in Siena's main square.

7 September – *Festa delle Rificolone* (Festival of the Chinese Lanterns): evening procession with torches and paper lanterns on Ponte San Niccolo and river banks.

The Florentine opera season gets underway in December and runs until April.

The highlight of the musical year is the celebrated *Maggio Musicale* festival (from mid-May to the end of June), which attracts some of the finest concert, ballet and operatic performers in the world.

Cinema and Nightlife

Almost all English language films screened in Florence have been dubbed into Italian. One place that shows movies in English is the Cinema Astro on Piazza San Simone. Note: many cinemas close for several weeks during the summer.

Florence has no shortage of lively bars, discotheques and night-clubs, all of which are enlivened by the large population of students and travellers. Again, the place to look for details of bands, films and so on, is the 'what's on' poster – there's usually one pinned up in the tourist office – or the weekend newspapers.

Sports

Swimming: you can swim or just sunbathe at the open-air pools of the Piscine Bellariva on Lungarno Colombo (ATAF bus 14), or the Piscine Pavoniere on Via degli Olmi, in the Cascine park (ATAF bus 16A).

There is a covered pool, Piscine Costoli, in the Campo di Marte sports complex (ATAF bus 3 or 10). To enjoy a dip in the sea, you'll have to travel to Viareggio, Forte dei Marmi, Marina di Pisa or Tirrenia, but you'll have to go even farther afield to find a really pleasant beach – north to Versilia, or south to the Gulf of Baratti. A small fee is usually charged for the use of beach facilities.

Tennis and golf: there are public tennis courts in the Viale Michelangelo and the Campo di Marte, as well as at the Campi dell'Ugolino, a golf-tennis-swimming complex, just south of Florence. The Ugolino also has an 18-hole golf course. The tourist office, which owns the latter establishment, will be happy to supply more details.

Walking: there are endless possibilities for fascinating walks in the rolling green hills that surround the city, and around places like Bellosguardo park, Fiesole, Certosa del Galluzzo monastery, Poggio Imperiale or the Arcetri observatory (which stands on the very hill from which Galileo gazed at the stars), all within easy reach of Florence. The tourist office supplies a useful map of the province of Florence, and will give all the advice needed on walking routes.

Italy is sports mad, and there is no shortage of facilities for both spectators and participants.

Children

Italians love children, and will make a fuss over them in hotels and restaurants, forgiving them any noise or nuisance they might cause.

Younger children quickly tire of museums and galleries, especially in the heat of summer. You can always intersperse museum visits with an ice-cream from the many *gelaterie* which line the streets in the city centre, or with a visit to a stylish Italian toy shop.

The sort of things children enjoy are the climbs to the top of the Campanile and the dome in the cathedral, or a visit to one of the more offbeat museums, such as the 'Specola' Natural History Museum, Via Romana 17, in the Oltrarno; the Anthropology Museum, Via del Proconsol 12; the Museum of Mineralogy, the Botanical Museum and the Museum of Geology and Palaeontology, Via La Pira 4.

One way to keep children amused is to have their portrait sketched by any of the artists or caricaturists who set up stalls around the Ponte Vecchio and the Uffizi.

If you're going to Florence for more than a few days, take at least one day off from sightseeing, and have a well-deserved **picnic** in the Cascine or in the hills around Fiesole (see p.76). You may also want to go to one of the city's swimming pools, or even escape to the coast for the day (see p.93).

A local bambino *enjoys a VIP view of a procession around the Piazza del Duomo.*

Eating Out

Tuscan cuisine has changed little since the time of the Renaissance, and many of the dishes you will find on Florentine menus of today were regularly served at the tables of the Medici. In Italy as a whole and Tuscany in particular, the emphasis is on straightforward, simply prepared country fare – no strong seasonings and no elaborate sauces.

The staples of the Tuscan kitchen are olive oil and bread. The **olive oil** produced in Tuscany is widely regarded as the finest in the world, dark green in colour, with a rich, peppery flavour. Local restaurants will display the brand of oil they use, in the same way that others might advertise their house wine, and local gourmets compare different oils like wine buffs discussing their favourite vintages. Tuscan olive oil is used in almost every dish, either as a seasoning or for frying, on salads, on bread, and poured generously over vegetables, soups and casseroles.

Your first taste of traditional Tuscan **bread** will reveal that it contains no salt. This eccentricity persists from the Middle Ages, when salt was a luxury item, and the thrifty Tuscans tried to cut back on its use. Bread is served with every meal, and is even a basic ingredient in many dishes – toasted and topped with a savoury *crostini* spread, diced and doused in oil as part of a bread salad, and especially in thick and hearty bread soups such as *pappa al pomodoro* and *ribollita* (see p.97).

A stroll through the busy food market situated near San Lorenzo will give you an idea of the fresh country produce that forms the basis of most Tuscan dishes: meat, poultry and game, especially wild boar and hare; plump tomatoes, peppers, artichokes and courgettes, and the ubiquitous local white beans; mozzarella, Parmesan, and the strong sheep's cheese known as *pecorino*; and delicious sweet figs, persimmons, several varieties of peaches, juicy lemons, and also crisp, cool watermelon.

Restaurants

Florence offers a wide range of eating places, from simple take-away pizza bars to high-class gourmet restaurants. The streets surrounding the main tourist attractions are packed with cafés, bars and pizzerias, where you can buy a snack. If you plan to eat in a café, remember that it is cheapest to eat standing at the bar – sitting at a table will cost more, while sitting outside on the terrace can be up to three times as expensive. Another option is the *tavola calda* (hot table), a self-service café where you can choose from a selection of pre-prepared dishes.

Restaurants range from the expensive *ristorante* to the more modestly priced family *trattoria*. Traditionally, the *trattoria* served basic fare in simpler surroundings than the more upmarket *ristorante*, but in Florence the distinction is somewhat blurred. All restaurants must, by law, issue a formal receipt indicating the sales tax or VAT (*IVA*). Theoretically, a customer may be stopped outside the premises and fined if unable to produce a receipt, so hang on to your bill! Cover (*coperto*) and service (*servizio*) charges are usually included, but if service is not included, leave about 10 percent for the waiter. All but the cheaper *trattorie* offer a three-course, fixed-price *menu turistico*, which is often a good deal, especially at lunchtime.

Meal Times

Breakfast (*prima colazione*) is usually included in the price of accommodation, and consists of a pastry or bread and jam washed down with copious amounts of coffee. It is served between 7.30am and 9.30am. **Lunch** (*pranzo*, *colazione*) is served from 12.30 to 2.30pm, though in the tourist-thronged centre of Florence, most places will serve food throughout the afternoon.

Dinner (*cena*) begins at around 7.30pm, and is traditionally a hearty affair of four courses: *antipasto* (appetizer), *primo* (soup or pasta), *secondo* (meat, game or fish, usually

Prime Tuscan beef provides the raw ingredient for the famous bistecca alla Fiorentina.

fried, grilled or roasted, and served unaccompanied except perhaps for a twist of lemon or a sprinkling of olive oil); and *dolci* (dessert). *Contorni* (side dishes) of vegetables or salad are ordered separately.

What to Eat

Antipasti (appetizers): among the usual Italian starters like the ubiquitous *antipasto misto* (a mixed spread of cold meats, sausage and cheese) and *mellone con prosciutto* (melon with ham), look out for local specialities like *prosciutto crudo con fichi* (raw ham with fresh figs), *crostini* (toast topped with a choice of savouries such as chicken livers, anchovies, capers, etc), *fettunta* (toasted country bread rubbed with garlic and sprinkled with olive oil), as well as *finocchiona* (a pork and fennel sausage).

Primi (first courses): traditional Tuscan soups include *pappa al pomodoro* (tomato and basil thickened with bread), *ribollita* (a bread-based vegetable soup, served cold in summer), *carabaccia* (thick onion soup), and *zuppa di fagioli* (a thick bean soup).

Pasta dishes are not a local speciality, but you will find *pappardelle alla lepre* (broad noodles with a sauce of wild hare), *ravioli con panna* (ravioli in fresh cream sauce), and *penne strascicate* (pasta quills in a ragu sauce), as well as *lasagne, spaghetti* and *tortellini* on the menu. Remember, you can order a half portion (*mezza porzione*) of pasta.

Other first-course dishes are *panzanella* (tomato, cucumber, bread and basil salad with olive oil), *risotto nero* (rice with squid cooked in its ink), and *cacciucco* (fish stewed in red wine, tomato and chilli).

Secondi (second courses): every visitor to Florence ought to try the famous *bistecca alla fiorentina*, a huge, charcoal-grilled T-bone steak, served with lemon, at least once. Each steak is around 2cm (1 inch) thick and weighs 600-800g (21-28oz), charred and crispy outside, rare and tender inside. It's sold by weight, and is always expensive. You will be shown your steak before cooking and told how much it weighs (the price per kilo is normally clearly marked on the menu). Not surprisingly, it's common for two people to share one *bistecca*.

Sophisticated salads grace the tables of the more expensive restaurants found in the city.

The other classic Florentine main course is *trippa alla fiorentina,* which is tripe, cut into thin strips, gently fried in olive oil with onion, celery, carrot, parsley and basil, then stewed for one hour with chopped tomatoes and a little wine, and sprinkled with grated Parmesan before serving.

Also on the menu are *fegato alla fiorentina* (sautéd liver flavoured with sage or rosemary), *arista* (roast loin of pork with rosemary and garlic), *fritto misto* (fried chicken, lamb, and rabbit with mixed vegetables), *peposo* (beef stew with a piquant sauce), and *stracotto* (casserole of beef with red wine and tomato).

Chicken turns up frequently on the Tuscan dinner table, cooked in several ways: *alla diavola* (charcoal-grilled); *arrosto* (roast); as *pollo alla cacciatora* (stewed with tomatoes and vegetables); or *petti di pollo saltati* or *fritti* (sautéd or fried breast). Hare and rabbit (*lepre* and *coniglio*) are commonly cooked *alla cacciatora*.

There's less emphasis on fish dishes, but two you're almost certain to find are *baccalà alla Livornese* (a stew of salt cod with garlic and tomato) and tasty *cieche alla pisana* (elvers cooked with garlic, tomato and Parmesan cheese).

Contorni (side-dishes): in Italy, vegetables (*verdure*) are usually served and charged for separately. Try *carciofini fritti* (fried artichokes), *frittata di carciofi* (artichoke omelette) or, in autumn, a plateful of grilled mushrooms (*funghi*). Typical Tuscan side-dishes are *fagioli all'uccelletto* (boiled white beans sautéd with tomato and sage), *fagioli al fiasco* (same ingredients, but baked), *fagioli all'olio* (boiled white beans, seasoned with oil, salt and pepper, and eaten almost cold), and *fiori fritti* (fried courgette flowers).

Dolci (desserts): fresh fruit (*frutta di stagione*) and ice-cream (*gelato*) are the most common desserts. Local specialities include Siena's *panforte*, a hard cake of fruit, nuts and spices, and *castagnaccio*, a paste of chestnuts, walnuts and raisins. Other sweets include the *zuccotto*, a liqueur-soaked sponge cake with chocolate and cream, and different kinds of *torta* (cake or tart). *Cantuccini* and *biscottini di Prato* are hard biscuits that you soften up by dipping into an accompanying glass of *vin santo*, a sweet dessert wine.

Picnics

If you fancy a change from restaurants and pizza bars, make up a picnic lunch and head for Fiesole, the Boboli Gardens, the Cascine, or the terrace of San Miniato, with all of Florence at your feet. Buy fresh fruit and bread from the market, then make for one of the many delicatessens (*pizzicheria*) in the surrounding streets. Crammed with mouthwatering merchandise, they stock a wide range of food and drink, including wine and soft drinks, and often sell sandwich rolls (*panino ripieno*). They'll usually oblige by filling your rolls with whatever you buy, saving you time and trouble.

The local market provides an abundance of edible goodies for a mouth-watering picnic lunch.

Picnics are the best way to sample some specialities you won't find so easily elsewhere. Try *finocchiona*, Tuscany's garlic- and fennel-flavoured salami, and don't neglect the wide range of Italian cured hams, salamis, *mortadella* sausages and other cold meats.

As for cheeses, try *stracchino*, *pecorino* (a tangy ewe's-milk cheese), *ricotta* (creamy cottage cheese), *caciotta*, *provola* (smoked or fresh), and, of course, *gorgonzola*, *parmigiano* and *grana* – the younger variety is eaten sliced rather than grated over pasta.

And **don't forget**: all food shops are closed on Wednesday afternoons.

Beating the Heat

At the height of summer, the heat in Florence can be overwhelming. Hot afternoons are best occupied by retreating to the shade of a café or *gelateria*, and nursing a cold drink or ice cream while you read, write postcards, chat, or watch the world go by. Though Florence as a whole suffers from a shortage of spacious open air cafés, there are a few upmarket establishments to try out in the Piazza della Signoria and Piazza della Repubblica.

You'll never be at a loss for a choice of thirst-quenchers in Florence, ranging from good Italian beers (*birra*) to iced tamarind juice (*tamarindo*), non-alcoholic bitters, freshly squeezed fruit juices (*spremuta*), iced coffee (*caffe freddo*), fruit milk shakes (*frullato*), and lemon juice poured over crushed ice (*granita al limon*). For children there's orangeade or lemonade (*aranciata* or *limonata*), and of course, a bewildering choice of delicious ice-creams (*gelato*).

Wines and Spirits

The traditional wine of Tuscany is **Chianti**, probably the best known of all Italian wines. Indeed, to many people outside Italy, Italian wine *is* Chianti – small wonder, perhaps, since Englishmen have been drinking it at home since the late 17th century. The wine is produced in the hills in the area of Florence, Pistoia, Pisa, Siena and Arezzo.

The picturesque and practical straw-covered *fiaschi* – the most famous wine bottles in the world – conjure up instant visions of Sunny Italy. With rising costs, this bit of folklore is sadly giving way to ugly plastic imitations (so hoard your *fiasco* for posterity!).

A light-bodied red wine, Chianti goes well with most kinds of food. Quality and price vary, but it's generally most acceptable and occasionally superb. If you're bent on trying a really fine Chianti from one of Tuscany's best vineyards, make sure the neck of your bottle bears a seal with the *Gallo Nero* (black cockerel) on it, the distinguishing mark of the Chianti *Classico* region between Florence and Siena. Bottles with a *Putto* (cherub) on the seal – the mark of the consortium representing the other Chianti regions – also guarantee authenticity and high quality.

Seven designated regions are allowed to use the name Chianti: Chianti *Classico*, *Rufina*, *Colli Fiorentini*, *Colli Senesi*, *Colli Aretini*, *Colline Pisane* and *Montalbano*. Tuscany produces a number of other light reds, however, including *Montecarlo*, *Brolio*, *Aleatico di Portoferraio* (from the Isle of Elba), *Vino Nobile di Montepulciano* (an unusual, slightly bitter red), and a fine dry red, *Brunello di Montalcino*; all are worth trying.

Among the few Tuscan white wines are the excellent dry *Montecarlo*, *Vernaccia di San Gimignano* and the mellow *bianco dell'Elba* (the Isle of Elba was for a long time a Tuscan possession, prized for its vineyards). From Elba, too, comes a range of white *spumante* (sparkling wines), just the thing to round off a celebratory meal.

If you have a passion for wine, join one of the several organized coach trips to the finest Chianti cellars, where you will be offered a tour of the wineries with their mighty oak casks and millions of bottles, ending with the opportunity to sample the produce. You can buy the wines you've tasted on the spot, often at extremely low prices. The tours take in some superb scenery and tourist attractions on the way (running from July to October, details available from the tourist information office).

Tuscans often like to end their meal with a small glass of

Vinsanto ('holy wine'), a deep amber-coloured sweet wine. If you're lucky enough to be invited to the home of a Tuscan friend, you'll almost certainly be welcomed with a glass of *Vinsanto*, whatever the time of day. Most bars and cafés, however, serve it by the glass.

Don't feel compelled to order wine with every meal; there's always the alternative of mineral water (*acqua minerale*), still or carbonated (*naturale* or *gasata*), or beer (*birra*). Florence's tap water is heavily chlorinated, but is nevertheless safe, if unpleasant, to drink.

You'll also have the opportunity to sample a wide range of aperitifs, digestifs and herb liqueurs, some of which are made by monks in nearby monasteries. *Sambuca* is an aniseed-flavoured liqueur often served flaming with three coffee beans floating on top; *Amaretto* is a sweet, almond-flavoured liqueur; *Strega* is a sweet, yellow liqueur sold in a tall bottle with a sprig of rosemary inside; and *grappa* is Italy's national firewater, distilled from the finely crushed seeds, skins and stalks left over from wine-making.

Lemon juice over crushed ice – granita al limon *– makes a great thirst-quencher in the hot weather.*

For a comprehensive glossary of wining and dining in Italy, ask at your bookshop for the comprehensive Berlitz EUROPEAN MENU READER.

To Help You Order ...

Good evening; I'd like a table.		**Buona sera; vorrei un tavolo.**	
Do you have a set menu?		**Avete un menù a prezzo fisso?**	
I'd like a/an/some …		**Vorrei …**	
beer	**una birra**	meat	**della carne**
bread	**del pane**	milk	**del latte**
butter	**del burro**	napkin	**un tovagliolo**
coffee	**un caffè**	potatoes	**delle patate**
cream	**della panna**	salad	**dell'insalata**
fish	**del pesce**	soup	**una minestra**
fruit	**della frutta**	spoon	**un cucchiaio**
fruit juice	**una spremuta**	sugar	**dello zucchero**
glass	**un bicchiere**	tea	**un tè**
ice-cream	**un gelato**	wine	**del vino**

... and Read the Menu

aglio	garlic	**maiale**	pork
agnello	lamb	**manzo**	beef
anitra	duck	**melanzana**	aubergine
baccalà	dried cod	**peperoni**	peppers
braciola	chop	**pollo**	chicken
calamari	squid	**prosciutto**	ham
carciofi	artichokes	**(crudo/cotto)**	(cured/cooked)
cipolle	onions	**risotto**	rice dish
coniglio	rabbit	**rognoni**	kidneys
fagioli	beans	**salsa**	sauce
fegato	liver	**sogliola**	sole
formaggio	cheese	**fragole**	strawberries
frittata	omelette	**stufato**	stew
frutti di mare	seafood	**triglia**	red mullet
funghi	mushrooms	**uova**	eggs
gamberi	prawns	**vitello**	veal

BLUEPRINT for a Perfect Trip

An A–Z Summary of Practical Information

Listed after most main entries is an appropriate Italian translation, usually in the singular. You'll find this vocabulary useful when asking for information or assistance.

A

ACCOMMODATION (*alloggio*)

(See also CAMPING on p.108, YOUTH HOSTELS on p.131 and the list of RECOMMENDED HOTELS starting on p.66)

Florence offers a wide range of accommodation, from luxury hotels and classic *pensiones* set in Renaissance palazzos, through more modest hotels and boarding houses to unclassified *pensiones* and guest houses with only basic amenities. Hotels are graded from one to five stars. The Florence Tourist Board (APT) (see TOURIST INFORMATION OFFICES on p.127) publishes an annually updated list of hotels, including details of prices and facilities.

In high season between March and October (and especially at Easter, in July and August, and during the annual fashion shows in March/April and October) Florence becomes very crowded and accommodation is at a premium. You are strongly recommended to book as far in advance as possible for this period. However, if you do find yourself in Florence without a hotel reservation, head for the Informazioni Turistiche Alberghiere (ITA) office in the Santa Maria Novella railway station (open daily 8.30am-9pm). For a fee of a few thousand lire they will find you a room within your price range.

Hotel prices are above average for Italy, and are on a par with other major European cities. Single rooms cost 60-70% of the rate for doubles. Prices must be clearly displayed in reception and in the rooms. Breakfast is often added on to the room rate automatically – if you do not want breakfast, make this perfectly clear before accepting the room.

I'd like a single/ double room.	**Vorrei una camera singola/ matrimoniale.**
with bath/shower	**con bagno/doccia**
What's the rate per night?	**Qual è il prezzo per una notte?**

AIRPORTS (*aeroporto*)

The main international airport for Florence is Pisa's **Aeroporto Galileo Galilei**, about 81km (51 miles) west of Florence. Facilities include a self-service restaurant, bar/café, post office, bank, 24-hour currency exchange machine, tourist information desk and car rental desks. For flight information, tel. (050) 500707. An hourly train service links the airport with Pisa Centrale (6 minutes) and Florence (one hour), between 7.40am and 11.40pm. The railway station is at the opposite end of the terminal building from the arrivals area – buy your ticket at the Information Desk. On your return journey, you can check in your bags at the Air Terminal on platform 5 (*binario 5*) at the railway station in Florence.

Florence's own small airport – Aeroporto Amerigo Vespucci – is at Perètola, 5km (3 miles) north west of the city. It handles mainly domestic flights, plus a few daily flights to major European cities. For flight information, tel. (055) 373948. A regular bus service connects the airport with the SITA bus station in central Florence, journey time 10-15 minutes.

Take these bags to the bus/ train/taxi, please.	**Mi porti queste valige fino all'autobus/al treno/al taxi, per favore.**
What time does the train for Florence leave?	**A che ora parte il treno per Firenze?**

B

BICYCLE HIRE (*noleggio biciclette*)

Bicycles can be hired from a number of outlets – the most central is a pavement stall (summer only) just off Piazza della Repubblica, at the corner of Via Calimali and Via Orsanmichele. You can also try Motorent, Via San Zanobi, 9r; tel. (055) 490113. Riding on the busy city streets can be hazardous, but there are pleasant paths along the banks of the Arno to the west of the town centre.

C

CAMPING (*campeggio*)

There is only one campsite convenient for the centre of Florence, with 240 pitches set on a pleasant hillside above the river east of Piazzale Michelangelo, 15 minutes' walk from the Uffizi. Contact *Italiani e Straniere* (Camping Michelangelo), Viale Michelangelo, 80, 50125 Florence; tel. (055) 681 1977. Reservations required.

There are several other campsites around the fringes of the city, and one in Fiesole. For details, contact the tourist office (see TOURIST INFORMATION OFFICES on p.127). There is also a free emergency campsite with very limited facilities for stranded backpackers, the Area de Sosta, on the edge of town. It is open in summer only, and the location sometimes changes from year to year. Ask at the tourist information office for the address of the current site.

May we camp here?	**Possiamo campeggiare qui?**
Is there a campsite near here?	**C'è un campeggio qui vicino?**
We have a tent/caravan (trailer).	**Abbiamo la tenda/la roulotte.**

CAR HIRE (*autonoleggio*)

(See also DRIVING on pp.113-116)

Although a car is not necessary for visiting Florence, Pisa and Siena, it gives you the freedom to explore many out-of-the-way places inac-

·essible by public transport. There are numerous car-hire firms n Florence and, if you're booking once in Italy, local firms often ·harge considerably less than the big international chains. Rates vary ·onsiderably, and you should shop around for the lowest price.

The best rates are usually found by booking and paying for your ·ar before you leave home, either directly through the office of an nternational rental company, or as part of a 'fly-drive' package deal. Check that the quoted rate includes Collision Damage Waiver, unimited mileage, and tax, as these can greatly increase the cost.

Normally you must be over 21 to hire a car, and you will need to ·ave held a full, valid driver's licence (EC model for EC citizens) for ıt least 12 months, which should be shown at the time of rental. You vill also need to show your passport and, ideally, a major credit card, ıs cash deposits are prohibitively large.

'd like to rent a car.	**Vorrei noleggiare una macchina.**

CLIMATE and CLOTHING

Florence's location, in a basin among the hills in the middle of the talian peninsula, means that it suffers from a more extreme climate han nearby coastal areas. Summer is often oppressively hot and ·ticky, while midwinter can be unpleasantly cold. Rain can fall at any ime of year, though it rarely lasts long in summer; the wettest nonths are from October to April. The best times to visit are in pring and autumn, when temperatures are less extreme, and the city s less crowded.

Approximate monthly average temperatures are as follows:

		J	F	M	A	M	J	J	A	S	O	N	D
°C	max	9	12	16	20	24	29	32	31	28	21	14	10
	min	2	2	5	8	12	15	17	17	15	11	6	3
°F	max	48	53	59	68	75	84	89	88	82	70	57	50
	min	35	36	40	46	53	59	62	61	59	52	43	37

Clothing. Lightweight cotton clothes are best for coping with the summer heat, but take along a sweater or jacket too for the cool evenings in spring and autumn. In winter, you will need warm clothes, a waterproof jacket and an umbrella. If you plan to do a lot of sightseeing, pack a pair of comfortable walking shoes.

Remember that Florence's churches are places of worship as well as works of art and architecture, and dress respectably if you intend to visit them – shorts, miniskirts and bare shoulders (a wrap or shawl comes in handy) are frowned upon.

COMMUNICATIONS

Post offices (*ufficio postale, PT*). The central post office in Florence is on Via Pellicceria, just south of Piazza della Repubblica. It handles mail, telegrams, telex and fax, and has a couple of coin- and card-operated public telephones. Stamps are on sale at counter 23, and from a machine just inside the entrance. Open 8am-7pm Monday-Friday, 8.15am-noon Saturday.

Postcards to EC countries cost L700, letters under 20g cost L750; postcards to the USA, L1,100, letters under 20g, L1,250. Aerogrammes to all countries can be bought for L850. Mail boxes are red – those marked *per la citta* are for destinations within Florence, *per tutte le altre destinazione* for all other destinations.

General delivery (*fermo posta*). It's not worth arranging to receive mail during a brief visit to Florence as Italy's postal system is notoriously slow. If you're going to be in Florence for a considerable time and must have things sent to you, there is a poste-restante (*fermo posta*) service at the Via Pellicceria post office (see above). Don't forget your passport for identification when you go to pick up mail (counters 32 and 24). Have mail addressed as follows:

Mr. John Smith
Fermo Posta
Palazzo delle Poste
Via Pellicceria
Florence, Italy

Telegrams, telex and fax. Service available at Via Pellicceria post office. Telegrams can be dictated by telephone, dial 186.

Have you received any mail for …?	**C'è posta per …?**
I'd like a stamp for this letter/postcard.	**Desidero un francobollo per questa lettera/cartolina.**
airmail	**via aerea**
registered	**raccomandata**
I want to send a telegram to …	**Desidero mandare un telegramma a …**

Telephones (*telefono*). You can make local and international calls from the orange public telephones located all over the city, which accept L100, L200 and L500 coins, and tokens called *gettoni*, worth L200. Many also accept phone-cards (*scheda telefonica*), which cost L5,000 and L10,000 and both phone-cards and *gettoni* can be bought from tobacconists (*tabacos*) and news-stands. Instructions for use are clearly displayed.

To make an international call, dial 00, followed by the country code (44 for UK, 1 for USA), then the area code minus the initial zero, and finally the number. Alternatively, to make a reverse charge or British Telecom Chargecard call to the UK, dial 172 0044 – this will put you straight through to a British operator (if you are using a public phone, insert L200 before dialling, which will be returned when you hang up the phone).

For enquiries, dial the following numbers, according to which country you are trying to reach:

Italy	**175**
Europe	**176**
Rest of the world	**1790**

Give me … *gettoni*/a telephone card, please.	**Per favore, mi dia … gettoni/una scheda telefonica.**

COMPLAINTS (*reclamo*)

Complaining is an Italian national pastime, but can involve elaborate bureaucratic procedures. Complaints should first be made to the management of the establishment concerned. If satisfaction is not obtained, threaten to take your matter to the regulating body, Provincia de Firenze, Via Cavour 37, 50129 Firenze; tel. (055) 293050.

To avoid problems, always establish the price in advance, especially when dealing with porters at stations. Any complaint about a taxi fare should be settled by referring to a notice, in four languages, affixed by law in each taxi, specifying extra charges (airport runs, Sunday or holiday rates, night surcharge) in excess of the meter rate.

CRIME

Florence is a fairly safe city, but you should take the usual precautions against theft – don't carry large amounts of cash, leave your valuables in the hotel safe, not in your room, and beware of pickpockets in crowded areas. Never leave your bags or valuables on view in a parked car. The main danger is from pickpockets, especially in busy markets and on buses. Beware of gypsy girls with babies or young children – while they distract your attention begging for coins, an accomplice will be behind you dipping into any available pockets and bags. If you have a shoulder bag, wear it across your body – it's harder to snatch.

Any theft or loss must be reported immediately to the police in order to comply with your travel insurance. If your passport is lost or stolen, you should also inform your consulate (see p.117).

I want to report a theft.	**Voglio denunciare un furto.**
My wallet/passport/ticket has been stolen.	**Mi hanno rubato il portafoglio/il passaporto/il biglietto.**

CUSTOMS (*dogana*) and ENTRY FORMALITIES

For citizens of EC countries, a valid passport or identity card is all that is needed to enter Italy for stays of up to 90 days. Citizens of Australia, New Zealand and the USA also require only a valid passport. For British tourists, a Visitors' Passport is sufficient.

Visas. For stays of more than 90 days a special visa or residence permit is required. Full information on passport and visa regulations is available from the Italian Embassy in your country (see EMBASSIES AND CONSULATES on p.117). Visa regulations change from time to time, and should be confirmed through your travel agent.

As Italy is part of the EC, free exchange of non-duty-free goods for personal use is allowed between Florence, the UK and Ireland. However, duty-free items are still subject to restrictions: check before you go. For residents of non-EC countries, restrictions when returning home are as follows: **Australia**: 250 cigarettes or 250g tobacco, 1l alcohol; **Canada**: 200 cigarettes and 50 cigars and 400g tobacco, 1.1l spirits or wine or 8.5l beer; **New Zealand**: 200 cigarettes or 50 cigars or 250g tobacco, 4.5l wine or beer and 1l spirits; **South Africa**: 400 cigarettes and 50 cigars and 250g tobacco, 2l wine and 1l spirits; **USA**:200 cigarettes or 50 cigars or 2kg tobacco, 1l wine or spirits.

Currency restrictions. Tourists may bring an unlimited amount of Italian or foreign currency into the country. On departure, however, you must declare any currency beyond the equivalent of L1,000,000, so it's wise to declare sums exceeding this amount when you arrive.

DISABLED TRAVELLERS

Many of the more popular attractions are equipped with ramps for wheelchair access, but public transport is a problem. Contact tourist information (see p.127) for details of accessible hotels, galleries and museums, and for addresses of Italian associations for the disabled.

DRIVING IN ITALY

Motorists planning to take their vehicle into Italy need a full driver's licence, an International Motor Insurance Certificate, and a Vehicle Registration Document. A Green Card is not a legal requirement, but it is strongly recommended for travel within Italy. Foreign visitors must display an official nationality sticker, and, if coming from the

UK or Ireland, headlamps must be adjusted for driving on the right. Full details are available from your automobile association, or from your insurance company.

The use of seat belts in front and back seats is obligatory; fines for non-compliance are stiff. A red warning triangle must be carried in case of breakdown. Motorcycle riders must wear crash helmets.

Driving conditions. Drive on the right, pass on the left. Give way to traffic coming from the right. Speed limits: 50kph/30mph in town, 90kph/556mph on highways, and 130kph/80mph on motorways.

The motorways (*autostrada*) and most major highways are excellent, skilfully designed for fast driving. There's often a lane to the extreme right for very slow traffic, especially on inclines. Florence lies near the famed *Autostrada del Sole* (A1), which runs the length of Italy, allowing fast road connections with Bologna, Milan, Rome and Naples. Italian *autostradas* are toll roads – you collect a card from an automatic machine when you join the motorway, and pay at the other end for the distance travelled. Try to stock up on coins, since the toll-booth attendants don't like sorting out change.

On country roads and many highways, you'll encounter bicycles, scooters, three-wheeled vehicles and horse-drawn carts. Those slow-moving vehicles rarely have lights, and are a danger after dark.

Traffic police (*polizia stradale*). Italian traffic police are authorized to impose on-the-spot fines for speeding and other traffic offences, such as driving while intoxicated or stopping in a no-stoping zone. All cities and many towns and villages have signs posted at the outskirts indicating the telephone number of the local traffic police headquarters or *Carabinieri* (see POLICE on p.125). Police have recently become stricter about speeding, an Italian national pastime. They also frown on the widespread practice of 'jumping the light'.

Should you be involved in a road accident, dial **112** for the *Carabinieri*. If your car is stolen or broken into, contact the Urban Police Headquarters (*Questura*) in Florence at Via Zara, 2 (see POLICE on p.125), and get a copy of their report for your insurance claim.

Petrol. Petrol is sold at set price levels. The grades available are *Super* (98-100 octane), *Normal* (86-88 octane), and *Senza Piombo* (unleaded – 95 octane – look for the pumps with green labels marked *senza piombo* or SP).

Driving in Florence. The centre of Florence (within the circle of avenues that surrounds it on both sides of the River Arno) is a restricted area, or *ZTL* (*zona traffico limitato* – limited traffic zone). This means that between 7.30am and 6.30pm Monday-Saturday, only residents who have a special permit on their windscreens are allowed into this zone. Traffic police are usually stationed at the major entry roads to stop anyone without a permit. Tourists are allowed to enter only to offload baggage and passengers at their hotel; you must then go and park outside the ZTL. If you can speak Italian, ask a policeman for directions, as the one-way system is rather complex.

Parking (*posteggio, parcheggio*). Even if you make it into the city centre after 6.30pm or on a Sunday, it is virtually impossible to park unless you can find space in one of the numerous official car parks. Parking in the street is generally reserved for residents. Apart from the city-centre parking places, there are others at Porta Romana (left bank), the Cascine (Piazza Vittorio Veneto) and Fortezza da Basso (Viale Filippo Strozzi). A smaller – but convenient – car park is located in Piazza Libertà.

If you park your car overnight in the centre of Florence, be careful to heed the parking time allowance. Parking fines are now very heavy and the city is equipped with trucks that remove illegally parked cars to the car pound (Parco Macchine Requisite, Via Circondaria, 19). If this should happen, call the pound (or ask your hotel to call, tel. 355231) to locate your car. You will then have to go there and pay a stiff fine to get it back.

Breakdown. In the event of a breakdown, find a telephone and dial **116**. This will put you in touch with the breakdown service of the ACI (*Automobile Club d'Italia*), the national motoring organization. Every 2km approximately (1½ miles or so) on the *autostrada* there's an emergency call box marked 'SOS'.

Road signs. Most road signs employed in Italy are international. Here are some written signs you might also come across:

Curva pericolosa	Dangerous bend (curve)
Deviazione	Diversion (Detour)
Divieto di sorpasso	No overtaking (passing)
Divieto di sosta	No stopping
Lavori in corso	Road works (Men working)
Pericolo	Danger
Rallentare	Slow down
Senso vietato/unico	No entry/One-way street
Vietato l'ingresso	No entry
Zona pedonale	Pedestrian zone
ZTL	Limited traffic zone
(International) Driving Licence	**patente (internazionale)**
car registration papers	**libretto di circolazione**
Green Card	**carta verde**
Can I park here?	**Posso parcheggiare qui?**
Are we on the right road for …?	**Siamo sulla strada giusta per …?**
Fill the tank please …	**Per favore, faccia il pieno de …**
super/normal	**super/normale**
lead-free/diesel	**senza piombo/gasolio**
I've had a breakdown.	**Ho avuto un guasto.**
There's been an accident.	**C'è stato un incidente.**

ELECTRIC CURRENT

220V/50Hz AC is standard. An adapter for continental-style two-pin sockets will be needed; American 110V appliances will also require a transformer.

an adapter	**una presa complementare**

EMBASSIES and CONSULATES

In Florence:

UK (consulate): Lungarno Corsini, 2; tel. (055) 284133

US (consulate): Lungarno Amerigo Vespucci, 38; tel. (055) 239 8276

In Rome:

Australia (HC): Via Alessandria, 215; tel. (6) 852721

Canada (HC): Via GB de Rossi, 27; tel. (6) 8415341

New Zealand (embassy): Via Zara, 28; tel. (6) 4402928

Republic of Ireland (embassy): Largo del Nazareno, 3; tel. (6) 6782541

South Africa (embassy): Via Tanaro, 14; tel. (6) 8419794

EMERGENCIES

If you don't speak Italian, find a local resident to help you, or talk to the English-speaking operator on the telephone assistance service, tel. 116 (see also Tourist Information Offices on p.127).

Police	112
General Emergency	113
Fire	115
Paramedics	118
Please, can you place an emergency call for me to the …?	**Per favore, può fare per me una telefonata d'emergenza …?**

police	**alla polizia**
fire brigade	**ai pompieri**
hospital	**all'ospedale**

ETIQUETTE

Italians do appreciate good manners. When you first approach the staff in a shop, restaurant or office, the expected greeting is always *buon giorno* (good morning) or *buona sera* (good afternoon/evening – from around 1pm onwards). When approaching anyone with an enquiry, start with *per favore* (please), and for any service rendered say *grazie* (thanks), to which the reply is *prego* (don't mention it, you're welcome). Introductions to men, women and older children are always accompanied by a handshake, the proper phrase being *piacere* (it's a pleasure). A more familiar greeting, used among friends and especially popular with younger people, is *ciao* (pronounced 'chow'), which means both 'Hi' and 'see you later'. In churches, shorts, miniskirts or bare shoulders are not considered respectable.

G

GAY and LESBIAN TRAVELLERS

Contact ARCI-gay, the national gay rights organization, tel. (051) 6447054 (office hours); or Lesbian Line, for advice and information, tel. (0551) 288126 (open 4pm-8pm Monday to Friday).

GUIDES and TOURS (*guida, viaggio*)

Most major hotels can arrange or provide multilingual guides or interpreters. Alternatively you can hire one independently through the Florentine Tourist Guides Society:

Soc. Coop. Giotto, Viale Gramsci, 9a; tel. (055) 247 8188

A number of travel agencies and bus companies offer organized tours of the countryside around Florence, and day-trips to Siena and

Pisa. Details can be obtained through your hotel, the tourist information office, and local travel agencies.

We'd like an English-speaking guide.	**Desideriamo una guida che parla inglese.**
I need an English interpreter.	**Ho bisogno di un interprete d'inglese.**

LANGUAGE (See also on the cover of this guide)

English is widely spoken in Florence, and you can easily get by without a word of Italian, but it is polite to learn at least a few basic phrases – Italian is an easy language to pick up. Local people will welcome and encourage any attempt you make to use their language.

The BERLITZ ITALIAN PHRASE BOOK AND DICTIONARY, covers most situations you are likely to encounter in your travels in Italy. The Berlitz Italian-English/English-Italian pocket dictionary contains some 12,500 entries, plus a menu-reader supplement.

LAUNDRY and DRY CLEANING (*lavanderia, tintoria*)

Launderettes and dry-cleaners in the town are worth seeking out because hotels charge extremely high prices. The 'Yellow Pages' directory (*Pagine Gialle*) lists addresses of establishments under 'Lavanderia' and 'Tintoria', or your hotel receptionist will tell you where the nearest facilities are. Coin-operated launderettes are rare; the usual practice is to leave the staff to do your washing, drying and folding for you, and to pick up your laundry later the same day.

When will it be ready?	**Quando sara pronto?**
I must have this for tomorrow morning.	**Mi serve per domani mattina.**

LOST PROPERTY (*oggetti smarriti*)

Ask for advice from your hotel receptionist or the local tourist information office before contacting the police. For items left behind on public transport, ask your hotel receptionist to telephone the bus or train station or taxi company. Lost property that has been handed in to the police has to be claimed at the City Council Lost Property Office (*Ufficio dei Oggetti Smarriti del Comune*), Via Circondaria, 19; tel. 367943.

I've lost my passport/ wallet/bag.	**Ho perso il passaporto/ il portafoglio/la borsetta.**

M

MEDIA

Newspapers and magazines (*giornale; rivista*). If you can read Italian, the Florence-based national newspaper, *La Nazione,* provides national and international news, features, and useful restaurant reviews and entertainment listings. *La Repubblica* also has a Florence edition. You can find British newspapers on city-centre newsstands, usually on the day after publication (*Guardian International* L2,200). The *International Herald Tribune* is available on the day of publication. A free booklet called *Concierge Information* is available from hotels and tourist offices, and contains a lot of handy information, including museum opening hours, train and bus timetables, as well as useful addresses.

Radio and TV (*radio, televisione*). The Italian state **TV** network, the RAI (*Radio televisione italiana*), broadcasts three TV channels, which compete with six independent channels. All programmes are in Italian, including British and American feature films and imports, which are dubbed. The airwaves are crammed with **radio** stations, most of them broadcasting popular music. The BBC World Service can be picked up on 648KHz AM.

MEDICAL CARE (See also EMERGENCIES on p.117)

EC citizens are entitled to free emergency hospital treatment if they have form E111 (obtainable from a post office before leaving home). You may have to pay part of the price of treatment or medicines; if so, remember to keep receipts so that you can claim a refund when you return home. Contact the Department of Health in your own country for further details.

Anything other than basic emergency treatment can be very expensive, and you should not leave home without adequate insurance, preferably including cover for an emergency flight home in the event of serious injury or illness. Your travel agent, bank, building society or insurance broker can provide a comprehensive policy which will cover not only medical costs, but also theft or loss of money and possessions, delayed or cancelled flights, and so on.

If you should need the services of an interpreter in a medical situation, contact the *Associazione Volontari Ospedalieri*, a group of volunteer interpreters who are always on call, and offer their services free; tel. (055) 403126 or 234 4567.

Most chemists (*farmacia*) are open during shopping hours, but some stay open all night. There's one in the main hall at the Santa Maria Novella railway station. On weekends or public holidays, the addresses of chemists on duty are published in the newspaper *La Nazione* and are also posted on every *farmacia* door.

No **vaccinations** are required for entry into Italy.

I need a doctor/a dentist.	**Ho bisogno di un medico/dentista.**
I've a pain here.	**Ho un dolore qui.**
a stomach ache	**il al di stomaco**
a fever	**la febbre**
sunburn/sunstroke	**una scottatura di sole/ un colpo di sole**

MONEY MATTERS

Currency. The unit of currency in Italy is the *lira,* plural *lire,* usually abbreviated to L or £. Coins come in denominations of 10, 20, 50, 100, 200 and 500 *lire,* banknotes in 1,000, 2,000, 5,000, 10,000, 50,000, and 100,000 *lire*. For currency restrictions, see CUSTOMS AND ENTRY FORMALITIES on p.112.

Banks and currency exchange offices. Banking hours are generally 8.30am-1pm and 3-4pm Monday-Friday. The exchange offices on Via dei Calzaiuoli, between the Duomo and Piazza della Signoria, are open all day and at weekends. There is also an exchange counter in the railway station, open 8.20am-7.20pm Monday-Saturday. Commission charges are often high, around L5,000 per transaction. The exchange counter at the post office in Via Pellicceria (see POST OFFICES on p.110) is open 8.15am-1pm Monday-Saturday and offers the best deal on transactions under L100,000.

Traveller's cheques and credit cards. In the main tourist areas, all banks, hotels and travel agencies, and many shops accept traveller's cheques, though you're likely to get a better exchange rate at a bank. Remember always to take your passport with you when you cash a traveller's cheque. Cash only small amounts at a time, and keep your remaining cheques in the hotel safe if possible. At the very least, be sure to keep your receipt and a list of the serial numbers of the cheques in a separate place to facilitate a refund in case of loss or theft. All the major credit cards are accepted by hotels, restaurants, car-hire firms and other businesses. If you have a PIN, you can also use your credit card to obtain *lire* from some Italian cashpoint machines; those have signs showing which cards they accept.

PLANNING YOUR BUDGET

To give you an idea of what to expect, here's a list of typical prices. These can only be regarded as approximate, as inflation continues to push costs upwards.

Airport transfer. Train (one-way) from Pisa Airport to Santa Maria Novella railway station in Florence, L6,500; to Pisa Central, L1,500.

Bicycle hire. L4,000/hour, L9,000/four hours, L15,000/24 hours.

Buses. ATAF tickets: 60 minutes, L1,100; 120 minutes, L1,500; 24 hours, L5,500; Carta Arancia, L25,000. SITA tickets: Florence-Siena return, L18,000.

Camping. Adult L6,000-7,000; child under 12, L4,500; car L4,000; caravan L9,000.

Car hire. *Group B* (Peugeot 106) unlimited mileage, inclusive of collision damage waiver and personal insurance (19-percent tax extra): L121,000 per day, L762,910 per week. *Group C* (Fiat Uno 1.2) unlimited mileage, inclusive of collision damage waiver and personal insurance (19-percent tax extra): L145,200 per day, L855,265 per week. A 10 percent tax is levied on cars picked up from the airport.

Food and drink. Lunch at café, L25,000 per person; dinner in a restaurant, from L40,000 up; take-away pizza slice, L2,500; ice-cream cone, L2,000-4,000; soft drink, L2,500; cappucino (at a café table), L3,000; freshly squeezed fruit juice (at a café table) L8,000; bottle of wine: in a restaurant from L8,000, in a shop from L4,000.

Hotels (double room with bath). 1-star L38,000-84,000; 2-star L62,000-110,000; 3-star L79,000-190,000; 4-star L180,000-282,000; 5-star L398,000-470,000.

Sightseeing. The Uffizi, L12,000; Palazzo Vecchio, L8,000; Museo Nazionale del Bargello, L8,000; Museo di San Marco, L8,000; Galleria Accademia (Michelangelo's *David*) L10,000; Galleria Palatina (Palazzo Pitti), L12,000; Giardino di Boboli, L5,000. Guided coach tour of Florence (3 hrs), L45,000; guided coach tour to Siena and San Giminiano (9 hrs 30 min), L58,000.

I want to change some pounds/ dollars/ traveller's cheques.	**Desidero cambiare delle sterline/dei dollari assegni di viaggio.**
Can I pay with this credit card?	**Posso pagare con la carta di credito?**

O

OPENING HOURS

Banks. 8.30am-1pm, and 3-4pm Monday-Friday.

Museums and art galleries. See p. 37.

Post office. 8am-7pm Monday-Friday, 8.15am-noon Saturday.

Shops. 8.30 or 9am-1pm, and 3.30 or 4-7 or 8pm. Most shops close all day Sunday, as well as Monday morning, except food shops, which close on Wednesday.

P

PHOTOGRAPHY and VIDEO (*fotografia, video*)

Major brands of film and video cassette are widely available, but they are expensive, so stock up before you leave. Photo shops in Florence can process your colour prints in 24-48 hours at reasonable prices, and some provide a 1-hour service. Protect your film from the heat, and never leave a camera or film lying in direct sunlight.

The use of flash or tripod is forbidden in most museums and cathedrals. Using a pocket camera in an art gallery may trigger the automatic flash, incurring the wrath of the gallery attendants – better to buy a postcard or reproduction, which will be of far better quality.

I'd like a film for this camera.	**Vorrei una pellicola per questa macchina.**
a colour-slide film	**una pellicola di diapositive**
a film for colour prints	**una pellicola per fotografie a colori**
How long will it take to develop this film?	**Quanto tempo ci vuole per sviluppare questa pellicola?**
May I take a picture?	**Posso fare una fotografia?**

POLICE (*polizia*)

Florence's city police, the *Vigili Urbani*, handle traffic, parking, and perform other routine tasks. While the officers rarely speak English, they are courteous and helpful towards tourists. The *Carabinieri*, a paramilitary force, wear light brown or blue uniforms with peaked caps, and deal with violent or serious crimes and demonstrations. Outside town, the *Polizia Stradale* patrol the highways, issue speeding tickets, and assist with breakdowns (see also DRIVING on p.113).

Vigili Urbani Headquarters (*Questura*) and Stolen Vehicles Department; tel. (055) 49771

Polizia Stradale (Traffic Police); tel. (055) 577777

Where's the nearest police station?	**Dov'è il più vicino posto di polizia?**

PUBLIC HOLIDAYS (*festa*)

Banks, government institutions, most shops and some museums are closed on national holidays, as well as on the Florentines' local holiday on 24 June, commemorating the town's patron saint, Giovanni Battista. During the week or ten days around 15 August, almost everything in Florence closes except hotels, a few shops, chemists, cafés and restaurants, and some of the major tourist attractions.

1 January	*Capodanno or Primo dell'Anno*	New Year's Day
6 January	*Epifania*	Epiphany
25 April	*Festa della Liberazione*	Liberation Day
1 May	*Festa del Lavoro*	Labour Day
15 August	*Ferragosto*	Assumption Day
1 November	*Ognissanti*	All Saints' Day
8 December	*Immacolata Concezione*	Immaculate Conception
25 December	*Natale*	Christmas Day
26 December	*Santo Stefano*	Saint Stephen's Day
Movable date:	*Lunedì di Pasqua*	Easter Monday

R

RELIGION (*religione*)

Italy is an overwhelmingly Roman Catholic country, with Catholicism accounting for 83% of the population. Mass is celebrated in English in the Duomo every Saturday at 5pm, and in the Church of San Giovanni di Dio, Borgo Ognissanti, 16-20, on Sundays and holidays at 10am. Many other denominations are represented in Florence; for details of services, contact the tourist information office (see TOURIST INFORMATION OFFICES on opposite page).

T

TIME DIFFERENCES

Italian time coincides with most of Western Europe – Greenwich Mean Time plus one hour. In summer, an hour is added for Daylight Saving Time, keeping it an hour ahead of British Summer Time.

New York	London	**Florence**	Sydney	Auckland
6am	11am	**noon**	8pm	10pm

What time is it? **Che ore sono?**

TIPPING (*mancia*)

Though a service charge is added to most restaurant bills, it is customary to leave a small additional tip for the waiter. If service charge is not included, 15% is the norm. It is also in order to tip bellboys, doormen, hat check attendants, garage attendants, and lavatory attendants a coin or two for their service. Taxi drivers do not expect a full 10%, and normal practice is simply to round up the fare. Tour guides generally expect 10%, and a few thousand lire should be offered to any custodian who goes out of his way to show you parts of a church that are normally closed to the public.

TOILETS (*gabinetto*)

You will find public toilets in airports, railway and bus stations, museums and art galleries; they are often designated by the sign 'WC'. The gents' may be indicated by 'U' (*uomini*), or 'signori', the ladies' by 'D' (*donne*), or 'signore'. Don't confuse *signori* and *signore!*

Where are the toilets?	**Dove sono i gabinetti?**

TOURIST INFORMATION OFFICES

The Italian State Tourist Office, or ENIT (*Ente Nazionale Italiano per il Turismo*), maintains offices in many countries throughout the world. A few are listed below:

Canada: 1 Place Ville-Marie, Suite 1914, Montreal H3B 3M9, Quebec; tel. (514) 866 7667

Ireland: 47 Merrion Square, Dublin 2; tel. (01) 766397

UK: 1 Princes Street, London W1R 8AY; tel. (071) 408 1254

USA: 500 N. Michigan Avenue, Chicago, IL 60611; tel. (312) 644 0990

630 Fifth Avenue, Suite 1565, New York, NY 10111; tel. (212) 245 4822

360 Post Street, Suite 801, San Francisco, CA 94108; tel. (415) 392 6206

In Italy, the provincial tourist information offices are the APT (Azienda di Promozione Turistica). They have English-speaking staff, and can provide free maps and give general advice and information. The APT offices in Florence and nearby are listed below:

Florence: Via A. Manzoni, 16; tel. (055) 23320 (8am-2pm Monday-Saturday)

Via Cavour, 1r; tel. (055) 290832 (8am-2pm Monday-Saturday)

Chiasso dei Baroncelli (a narrow alley to the right of the loggia), Piazza della Signoria (8am-7.30pm daily in summer, 9am-3pm Monday-Saturday in winter)

Fiesole: Piazza Mino, 37; tel. (055) 598720
(8.30am-6.30pm Monday-Saturday)

Siena: Piazza del Campo, 56; tel. (0577) 280551
(8.30am-7.30pm Monday-Saturday)

Pisa: Piazza Statione; tel. (050) 42291
(9.30am-noon, 3-5.30pm, closed Sunday afternoon and Monday morning)

Piazza Duomo; tel. (050) 560464
(9.30am-noon, 3-5.30pm, closed Sunday afternoon and Monday morning)

TRANSPORT

Buses. The orange ATAF buses provide a cheap and efficient way of getting around the city and its suburbs. Buy your ticket before you board from automatic ticket machines at the main bus stops, or from shops and news-stands displaying an orange BIGLIETTI ABBONAMENTI ATAF QUI ('bus passes here') sign, and cancel it in the machine on the bus. Tickets are valid for one, two or 24 hours, and you can make as many journeys as you like, as long as they begin within the period of validity (you only punch the ticket once, on the first bus you use). Tourists can also buy a *Carta Arancio* (Orange Card), which gives seven days' unlimited travel on buses and trains within the province of Florence (this does not include Pisa or Siena). For details of timetables and routes, call at the ATAF information office outside the railway station, or tel. (055) 580528.

A number of other bus companies provide inter-city services to destinations further afield, including Siena, Perugia, Rome, and Milan. The main companies are SITA, tel. (055) 211487, whose station and information office is in Via Santa Caterina da Siena; Lazzi, tel. (055) 298840, in Piazza Stazione, opposite the railway station; and COPIT, tel. (055) 215451, in Piazza Santa Maria Novella. The *Carta Arancio* can also be purchased from any of these ticket offices.

Taxis. Taxis can be picked up at ranks in the main city squares, or called by telephone (tel. 4242, 4798, or 4390). Fares are recorded on the meter, and there are extra charges for luggage, station pick-ups, and late-night trips. It is normal practice to round up the fare.

Trains. The Italian State Railway, FS (*Ferrovie dello Stato*), has an excellent rail network, though the system is complicated, and the slower trains are often late. Florence's Santa Maria Novella railway station is well-designed and efficient, with regular services to Rome, Milan, Venice, and other European cities. In addition to the information desks, there are a number of computerized information points, where you can get train times and fares from a touch-screen terminal. Prices are fairly cheap. Ticket machines take credit cards as well as cash. The most useful rail service for visitors is the hourly train to Pisa, convenient for a day-trip to see the Leaning Tower.

When's the next bus/ train to ...?	**Quando parte il prossimo autobus/treno per ...?**
single (one-way)/ return (round-trip)	**andata/ andata e ritorno**
first/second class	**prima/seconda classe**
What's the fare to ...?	**Qual è la tariffa per ...?**

TRAVELLING TO FLORENCE

BY AIR

Scheduled flights. From Great Britain, British Airways and Alitalia offer daily direct flights from Heathrow to Pisa, the nearest international airport to Florence, with connecting flights from all parts of the UK. The only direct flight from Britain to Florence's own airport at **Peretola** is the daily Air UK service from Stansted. The best deal on scheduled flights is the APEX fare, which must be booked at least 14 days in advance, and include a Saturday night abroad.

From the **USA**, there are dozens of scheduled flights from the major American cities to the international gateway airports of Rome and Milan, where you can catch a connecting flight to Pisa or Florence. Numerous charter flights and package deals are available – check with your travel agent for the latest deals.

Charter flights and package tours. Package tours featuring Florence are numerous, ranging from stays of four to 14 nights. Most package tours are on a room only or room and continental breakfast basis. A few provide half-board, but at a supplement. Flights go from Gatwick or Heathrow, and the main Italian operator also offers a rail-package deal departing from London's Victoria Station. Florence is also featured as part of two-centre packages in conjunction with Rome and the Tuscan resorts and hills, or the Italian Lakes.

It is also possible to get a seat on a charter flight on a flight-only basis, which is usually much cheaper than a ticket on a scheduled flight. However, charters are less flexible, with perhaps only two flights weekly, and there are restrictions attached which should be checked out at the start. Cancellation insurance is recommended.

BY ROAD

A coach service runs three times a week from London Victoria to Florence, taking 32 hours. For drivers taking their own vehicles, the fastest route from the channel ports is via Paris and the A6 Autoroute du Soleil to near Macon, then east on the A40 and through the Mont Blanc Tunnel to Turin, Genoa and finally Florence.

BY RAIL

The most direct rail route from Britain is the daily boat train from London Victoria to Paris, where you change to the overnight train to Florence, arriving the following morning. The journey takes 22 hours, and the ticket is only slightly cheaper than travelling by air. If you are touring Europe by rail, the following passes can be used in Italy: *Inter-Rail*, *Rail Europ Senior*, *Eurailpass*, *Eurail Youthpass*.

Italian State Railways offer fare reductions in certain cases. The BTLC Tourist Ticket (*Biglietto Turistico di Libera Circolozione*) is valid for specified periods of unlimited travel within Italy in first or second class, and the Kilometric Ticket (*Biglietto Chilometrico*) can be used by up to 5 people for up to 20 journeys totalling a maximum of 3,000 person-km (ie. 1,500km each for two people, 600km each for five). These tickets can be purchased at home or in Italy.

W

WATER (*acqua*)

There are numerous old drinking fountains in Florence's parks and piazzas. Tap water is safe, but mineral water is more palatable.

a bottle of mineral water	**una bottiglia di acqua minerale**
still/fizzy	**naturale/gasata**

WEIGHTS and MEASURES

Temperature

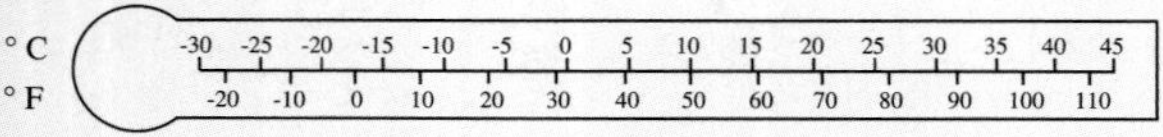

Length

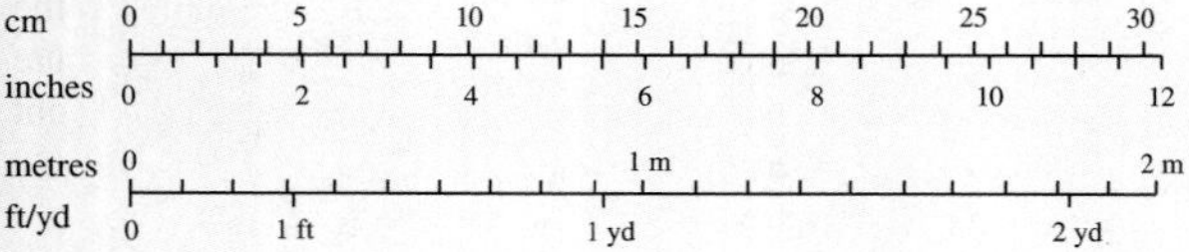

Weight

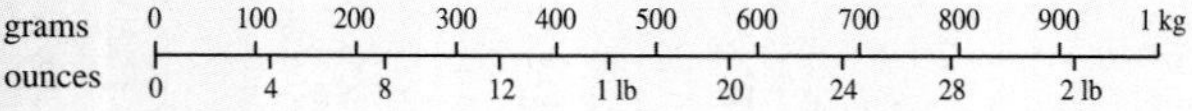

Y

YOUTH HOSTELS (*ostello della gioventù*)

Contact your national youth hostel association before departure to obtain an international membership card. The Italian Youth Hostel Association (*Associazione Italiana Alberghi per la Gioventù*) has one hostel on the outskirts of Florence, a 30-minute bus trip from the centre: Ostello Villa Camerata, Viale Augusto Righi, 2; tel. 601451.

Index

Where there is more than one set of references, the one in **bold** refers to the main entry, the one in *italic* to a photograph.

039/506 SUD